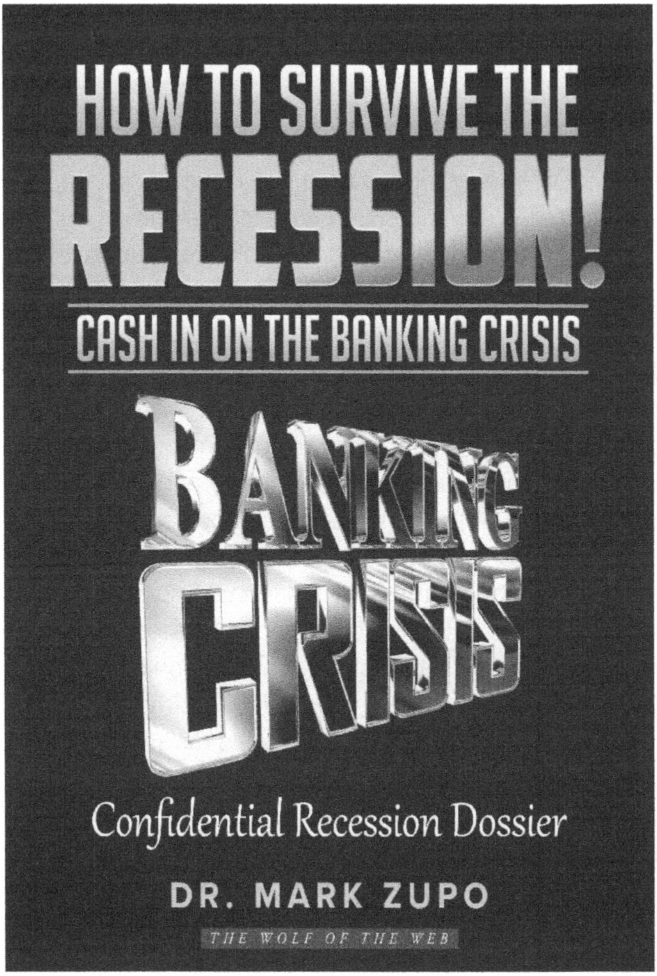
HOW TO SURVIVE THE
RECESSION!
CASH IN ON THE BANKING CRISIS
BANKING
CRISIS
Confidential Recession Dossier
DR. MARK ZUPO
THE WOLF OF THE WEB

**The Banking Crisis**
**Confidential Recession Dossier**



**ISBN-10: 0-9964000-4-4**
**ISBN-13: 978-0-9964000-4-6 (Mark Zupo)**
**LCCN: 2021924179**
Printed in the Unites States of America
**10 9 8 7 6 5 4 3 2 1** --- Launch!

# How To Survive The Recession

## Cash In On The Banking Crisis™

## "CONFIDENTIAL" RECESSION DOSSIER

**Dr. Mark Zupo**

**DEDICATION**

This is dedicated to every working slob and slob-ette out there who has had enough of the boss, time clocks, night shifts, layoffs, downsizing, discrimination, office politics, low pay, and trading hours for dollars.

Chin up, chest out, shoulders back and eyes forward.

I grant you "empowered" to be in control of your life
from this moment on.

**Go for it!**

## FORWARD

Contagion. This refers to the characteristic shock that takes place when the financial systems, nationally and globally, as a recession occurs. This is usually the result of the powers that be, failing to protect the consumers and tax-payers in this country when they play with our economic system. Who suffers? We do.

Past banking crises have been instrumental to our understanding of the systemic risk we take when we challenge the norms and play with the vulnerability of the capitalist system. Market fluctuations, trade wars, interest rates, economic stimulation, increased prices, decreased buying power, embezzlement, poor management, and other tender phenomenon usually result in the collapse of financial systems and leave the people with huge risk, loss, burden, volatility, and a turbulent life from the onset.

At the heart of the problem are the Banks. They are fragile businesses, emphasis on businesses, that are federally regulated but subject to erroneous information, depositor misinterpretation, money manipulation, bailouts, panic, inflation, bubbles, ruined economies, political manipulation, credit ruining monsters, higher public debt and more. They are an equal-opportunity menace.

The first recorded episode of banks in trouble was in the 1800's. It has grown to gargantuan size up to the present century. The panic in 1907, World War I, the Great Depression in the 1930's, the oil embargo of 1974, the Mortgage and housing bubble and crisis in 2007-2008, (which lasted for more than 10 years!), and the current trade wars are all well remembered as devastating to the people. Us. Those most vulnerable to any fluctuation in the cash flow income system.

The banking crisis problem has become a serial concern. It happens no matter what we do individually but affects us all collectively. It happens more than you think, and we are always caught with our "pants down" when it does. Why? Because we are in denial. We don't prepare for it. We're never ready for it and we are caught up in making a living trading dollars for hours instead of working to earn money.

The sub-prime mortgage crisis caught me red handed. I lost $3-Million dollars cash. I was $12-Million dollars in debt, financially ruined, unemployed, bankrupt, foreclosed, homeless, out of business and coincidently, widowed at the same time. To the point, I was invested in Real Estate heavily. That included mortgages, construction and so on. It was my ONLY stream of income. A HUGE mistake and the single-most important topic of this book.

As for the details and specific resources I've used here, I speak in generalities for the references I make here. You can look up anything to verify what I say is and was real. Unless of course…you experienced it personally like I did!

How do we know there is a crisis looming in our future? All signs point to it. Complicated but revealingly simple signs. We are ignoring most of them as usual. We ignore them because we are comfortable now as we have experienced job growth, higher income opportunity that goes with the job market and increased spending in services. We feel good about housing process, increased minimum wages, more jobs because of employer confidence and more.

However, the truth is that we have so quickly forgotten that we also are paid less and taking lower-paying jobs because we need any income after the 2008 debacle. The same job that paid a premium ten years ago now pays about 50% less, decreased benefits and no future longevity promise like there used to be. Capitalism, you gotta love it don't you?

We accept less because we are trained to accept what we are given or offered. Our money is worth less and NOT backed by gold. We become a slave to credit cards and reverse mortgages as offered to the older population. Whomever said, " there's a sucker born every minute" could not be righter...or is there?

This book will help you NOT to be that "SUCKER". There is a way to fend off the creditors and become the person who starts now to build resources so that when it happens, the banking crisis, like before, you will have what you need to survive and...survive comfortably.

Nothing in this book is a secret and we already know everything that I will restate. Sometimes we just need to be reminded and enlightened. There are no guarantees, but there are possibilities.

I'm ready, are you?

**Selected Categories**

Nonfiction > Business & Economics > Banks & Banking

Nonfiction > Business & Economics > Decision-Making & Problem Solving

## CONTENTS

## ACKNOWLEDGMENTS

I acknowledge that I know very little.
I acknowledge that I will make mistakes.
I acknowledge that I am open to learn more.
I acknowledge that I will correct my mistakes.
I acknowledge that I know enough to be dangerous.
I acknowledge that I have questions with no answers.
I acknowledge that I have humility, dignity, and respect.
I acknowledge that I am empowered to share what I know.

I acknowledge that I am your servant to help you succeed.

# Introduction

## What is happening in the world today?

I'll tell you what I know and what I think you should know immediately. There is a crisis happening in the United states right now that has caused fuel prices to skyrocket, people losing their homes, people losing their jobs, people being forced to do things against their will, inflation through the roof, and people spending less money because they have to tighten their belts.

Inflation alone is hit people very hard. We are earning less money; the money is worth less and products are stacked up by the hundreds of thousands unable to get to the consumers. There aren't enough people to unload ships and aren't there enough people to drive the product's over the road to the consumers. Compact has been tremendous. And it looks like there is no stopping it! So, one has to ask the question, why?

Every day now we are as much concerned about our safety and security for our family considering what is happening in America today. More and more businesses are closing by the day. Entrepreneurs cannot afford to continue to run their “Mom and Pop” businesses under the pressure of a failing economy with no end in sight.

I'm afraid and you should be too!

It doesn't take a genius to recognize that there's a news story every five minutes about stores closing, gas prices rising, companies are outsourcing business to Mexico and China, people are losing their jobs, people are quitting their jobs and companies are laying off employees and blaming it on automation.

What you don't hear about or the many thousands of people behind the scenes who are benefiting from this recession and betting on the recession to make them even more money. At this point I think it's very important that everyone know just exactly what's going on because you have the right to know.

What we will face in the next few months or even the next couple of years will be a future that is much different that we know now. That's my job in this book, because one single individual cannot change the system but every single individual needs to know how to prepare for it. It is crucial that the information in this book is in your hands as soon as possible because there will be opportunities right now for you to make changes before the unthinkable happens.

Even with the bad news surrounding you 24 hours a day seven days a week, you might still be confident that your financial future is OK. The problem with that line of thinking is there is huge economic turmoil happening behind your back.

I can tell you with absolute surety and from personal experience that I was completely confident in my financial future in 2006. At the beginning of 2007 there were signs on the horizon that something big was going to happen, but it wasn't made public for fear of a run on the bank and people pulling money out of their retirement.

The contrast between where I was in 2006 and where I was in 2008 is a crevasse deeper than the ocean and I never saw it coming. As of today, Americans have fallen behind in their bills, lost homes to foreclosure, I found it necessary to file bankruptcy and generally feel insecure about their future.

According to surveys done by The US board of economics, just under 60% of people in retirement cannot afford to live on the meager income from Social Security. The average American does not have $3000 in savings and could not survive more than 60 days without income for food and housing.
However, do not despair. There are several solutions that I will highlight in this book that you absolutely must take advantage of before it's too late.

Don't wait till the last minute to prepare. Pay attention and learn about how you're being treated and who has your back. I can assure you; it is not your bank.

Fact, as I have and will state many times throughout this book, banks are not your friend. The Federal Reserve is not your friend. And the collapse of one single bank in the United states can trigger the collapse of many banks in less than three days. considering that most of the small banks have been bought up and are now owned by the three or four largest banks in the country attests to the lack of control that you have and the huge amount of control that they have.

We are currently in a recession, that will rival the Great Depression of 1932. We are headed for national collapse of our banking system and creditworthiness across the globe. Be forewarned, digital currency is taking over because the government does not want cash in the hands of Americans because it represents a power they cannot control. Once banking has gone entirely digital, you will have zero control over your life.

There is a war on cash. Your cash. And if the powers that be decide they want to confiscate your cash come along with it they will take your liberty and then be able to track every dollar you spend and every dollar you earn.

There is huge evidence that this is occurring right now under your nose and behind your back and unfortunately right in front of you. The problem is we are so busy making a living that we are blinded by the stresses and mandates that we are subject to. In the United States of America, there are powerful forces that are not working for your benefit but to your detriment. And once your earning power is gone or under the control of someone else cash will disappear and so will your liberty.

Have you ever been to a restaurant or a business that will not take cash? Have you ever been told by a business that they won't use a certain credit card? How difficult is it to buy an airline ticket without a credit card? What happens if you make a deposit or withdraw over $10,000?

Do you know that if you have cash in your car, that when stopped by a police officer, they can confiscate your cash because it represents at someone carrying too much cash can be suspected of terrorism for drug dealing. My goal for this book is to give you the opportunity to wake up and smell the money.

I hope this book will do three things for you.

1. Give you the opportunity to see what's happening around you and why you should be scared
2. To impress upon you a sense of urgency and give you some guidance and direction about what actions to take before the recession cripples our economy.
3. To give you some education and understanding of how your bank controls you and every other aspect of your life. Especially before it all comes crashing down.

The banks, can and will, seize your money and your assets and they don't even have to tell you about it until it's too late.

The title of this book is cash in on the banking crisis. That is on purpose to give you an idea but what you will find in this book about saving what you have, protecting what you have and making out better than you were before you read my book.

**There has never been a more important time in the history of The United states,** and very likely the entire planet, if we don't make ourselves aware, and educate ourselves into the failings of the people that elect to lead us.

This book, how to survive the banking crisis, is the first in the series of 40 books that will look carefully at the conditions that will exist if we don't learn our lessons. At the end of this book, I will give you a list of the forthcoming books that will open your eyes to what the future has to hold for you. I beg you, buy them, read them, and carry them so you will not be caught by surprise.

## Psychological Reactions

It is important for the communicator to understand that in crisis, people often manifest the following psychological reactions:

- Vicarious rehearsal
- Denial
- Stigmatization
- Fear and avoidance
- Withdrawal, hopelessness, and helplessness

## The 3 Types Of Crisis

Creeping **Crises** – foreshadowed by a series of events that decision makers don't view as part of a pattern.

- Slow-Burn **Crises** – some advance warning before the situation has caused any actual damage.

- Sudden **Crises** – damage has already occurred and will get worse the longer it takes to respond.
- Creeping **Crises**.

**The Four Stages of a Crisis**

Stage 1: Prodromal (**Pre**-Crisis)
Stage 2: Acute (Crisis)
Stage 3: Chronic (Clean-Up)
Stage 4: Crisis Resolution (Post-Crisis)

**Crisis Intervention 101.**

There are six **stages** within every **crisis**: (1) warning; (2) risk assessment; (3) response; (4) management; (**5**) resolution and (6) recovery. This is the fifth of six topic briefings to explore a specific **crisis stage**, identify the specific issues of that **stage** and provide manageable solutions.

**Crisis Cycle**. We all experience stressors that lead to escalation. This **cycle** is typically referred to as the **Crisis Cycle**. By following basic recommended responses, you can minimize the time and intensity of each episode. An awareness of each phase and possible responses promotes better outcomes for all involved.

# Chapter 1

# Danger – Banks Ahead!

I am fairly certain that The United states economy and banking system is about to collapse, and it will be worse than what was experienced in 1932.

We are now experiencing shortages; supply chain issues credit issues trade wars and it is ready to blow sky high. There is little that anyone can do about it other than prepare for themselves.

There has been an economic crisis in this country behind the scenes that started in 2019 and is now picking up speed. It is not just about the elite, but it is more concerning for the average American middle-class family. the banks are preparing to close in on what little wealth you have, if any.

We have been gouged by increasing prices on everything a shortages on everything else. And the banks are preparing to take away the rest of what we have. Don't take my word for it. The banks have a purpose, and that purpose is to control the highest tax paying group in the country, The middle class of the United States of America. It's not a secret. The goal for the Fed is to eliminate currency, engage with digital money and use your personal information against you.

The single most untrustworthy business in the world power banks. They are unsafe. Not long ago, the government bailed the banks out because of the savings and loan crisis. When was the last time you were bailed out when you got into financial trouble? Oh, never, that's right.

Billions of dollars were invested in a banking system that lost control and wiped out all of the equity and capital of many thousands of people. They simply said, we don't have it anymore. Because of the events of 2007. The lack of money that was actually not in the bank help to reveal a great number of Ponzi schemes and embezzlement schemes that put many people in prison. Interestingly, we had absolute faith in those people that we trusted our money to.

Why is that?

Because we have been taught since birth that we are worker bees and should be happy in our labor and happy giving a portion of what we earn to the government to tell us we should be happy in our labor.

There have been more than 50 banks that have declared bankruptcy and have closed because no one was paying attention. It was the rule of law that credit and rates were compromised to help the American people get back on their feet.

The FDIC, the Federal Deposit Insurance corporation, was supposed to ensure the money against loss. Auditors and many academics worked tirelessly to try and maintain the stature of a bank. They do that because the regulatory agencies that supervise the banks are supposed to pay close attention to how a bank operates.

It seems that, even the government doesn't trust the banks that they monitor. Bank scandals have been sweeping through The United states economy for more than 100 years. Embezzlement, money laundering, Ponzi schemes, another nefarious activities hangs the credibility of banks out to dry.

Does your bank have a well-recognized name? Is your bank one of the big three in the United states? If it is then you should be more worried than anybody else. they are the most notorious The global market is supported by fear and greed and emotion. How trustworthy does that sound?

Banks use a system that is nothing short of stealing. When you make a deposit they put about 20% of you are money in the bank. The idea is that they expect no more than 20% of the people to clear the money out of the bank at any one time. So where does your money go? When there is a recession and depositors begin to panic, the bank Is no longer fluid and can refuse to give you your money because... they really don't have it.

So, what happened to the other 80% of the money? If you have ever seen the movie with Jimmy Stewart, you would know that the building and loan used it to help other people buy a house or start a business. How the bank makes money is on the interest that they charge for those services. It doesn't sound like that would be very much, however get totals in the billions of dollars.

Just wait, we're coming to the good part where you get screwed royally with a smile.

There is another term for money that doesn't exist called Fiat money. Just wait till I tell you about that. Bankers make sure that in the process of doing business they leverage themselves to an unbelievable amount. There is no other business in the world leveraged as much as banks are. Even though banks are worth billions of dollars in this country alone, they actually lose more money than they make! Let that sink in.

That's the reason for all of the excess charges that you get from a bank for servicing fees, bounce checks, fraud, embezzlement, and downright underhanded business. some simple math might bring that into focus. Banks take your money and pay you a measly interest on your savings. thanks then loan your money out at high interest rates that they don't control. The Fed does that.

Sometimes the Fed, raises their rates and sometimes

the Fed lowers the rates. And the banks have to adjust. The difference between the two is called the spread. It is January around 8% of the profit they make and that is what they used to run the banks. I'm not feeling sorry for the banks but imagine having to run your household on 8% of what you earn!

The greater portion of the interest rate that you pay is for the risk that the bank takes in lending you money. Usually, it's your own money that they borrow to lend you money. Sounds confusing doesn't it? Well, it's easily as untrustworthy a business model.

Right behind that comes inflation. That's usually a product of a recession.

All that adds up to your dollar being worth about $0.75 to buy $0.85 worth of product. That my friends is inflation. A very scary scenario. Generally, the money that is lent for unverified collateral like the home that was built for $60,000 selling for $300,000 and then losing that value by 50% when people get scared, and you know what starts to hit the fan.

Another big consideration is when people do not pay back the money they agreed to when they took out a loan and the bank has to cell a worthless property that they took from you to recover what they lost. They do so by charging higher interest rates. The problem with that is that that is controlled by the Fed. That is how they control the money supply and keep you right where you are.

Have you ever heard of eminent domain? That's where the government take your land property and uses it to build a highway through your house. And to be fair, they pay you what they think it is worth. And surely you understand that you will not come out on the best side of that.

Another means of control. So, what is the solution? Keep reading and I will get to that.

So, what happens when inflation takes a big bite out of your earnings? The Fed raises the interest rate and charges more to slow down spending. That's when the banks become money launderers. Even though the money supply is not controlled by the banks it is certainly managed and manipulated by the banks. To their favor.

*NOTE - You need to know this information so I will not apologize for some basic education that I have detailed so far. It's very important to know exactly what's going on so that we can find a way to fix it. While we're keeping you out of the poor house.

So, as I explained before, the control of all this and your money becomes irrational unrealistic. As we screw with our money, the banks affect foreign countries as well which starts another ball rolling that costs you dearly. This lack of trust in the banks, reduces morale and credibility and the effect is that people get scared. That's when you know that your money in the bank, any bank is not safe.

In 2008 I lost my home and all my property, my cars, my business, and my savings. All of those things were immediately confiscated when I indicated that I would have to file bankruptcy. My home was worth 50% of what I had invested in it. I could not sell it and was forced to let it go back to the bank in foreclosure.

Just to make something clear here, no one asked me or told me that they were going to seize my assets. And it happened faster and the speed of light. You think you're safe? Trust me when I say you are not safe you can be in the street in as little as three days. Because I had a variable interest rate on the mortgage of my home, when the mortgage crisis happened the interest rate doubled and so did my payment. It was more than I make in two weeks. So, the choice was live in the home and not be able to eat or feed my family or let the home go back to the bank in foreclosure and bear the brunt of bankruptcy.

by the way, guess what happens to the interest rate on your credit cards when you can't pay the loan immediately worth default on the loan by buying more than you can afford to pay for? The interest rates skyrockets to an unbelievable amount that make it nearly impossible for you to pay anything and ever catch up or ever pay off the loan on the credit card for the things that you've purchased. In other words, you have taken out a loan by buying something on the trust of your credit on a credit card and you can pay for it overtime and pay an interest rate based on how long you borrow that money against your purchases.

**Back to the banks**.

Since the federal government is the only entity that has permission to print money, cash, the banks aren't permitted to do it, so they have to find another way to make money. As of today, there is electronic and digital cash and virtual cash that they can manipulate without the government interfering.

**Bingo! You've been screwed again**. Are you getting used to it yet? There has been a great deal of turmoil in Washington that nearly ended in a complete shutdown of the government. I am not completely antigovernment however it is important to understand that like a contagion, what goes on in Washington that you are not aware of is usually the very thing that will hurt you the most.

the stock market goes up and the stock market goes down based on a simple comment or tweet by a president can you either make a dollar or two or lose hundreds of dollars or two. It makes it difficult for anyone to keep up with what happens on a daily basis. We won't even start talking about how much this country is in debt.

The national debt is skyrocketing, and it seems as though nobody cares.

**The economic collapse is right around the** corner. You don't hear a great deal about it because the government wants you to trust in them and not be frightened about the possibilities.

**And it starts with the banks.** When it happens, it's going to happen fast. There won't be much warning. The things that keep the financial economy safe will fail. There aren't many safeguards to prevent that from happening.

We got a glimpse of that in 2008. There was just under $200 billion in the bank and a panicked middle class tried to take it all out at one time. Some of the biggest businesses in the world went bankrupt. People showed up for work and the doors were locked. We came very close to running out of food, the supply chain failed, fuel for aviation and business came to a grinding halt.

When it happens, your personal line of credit goes out the window. Credit cards are no longer valuable and of course the banks will close their doors to you. If it gets bad enough during the collapse, your local governments will close their doors as well. That means when the pumps stop there won't be any more water. That means when the electrical generators stop there won't be any more electricity.

After that, the more serious businesses like communications and emergency services may stop as well. Do you think it might be important to have cash on hand? Your credit card will be worthless. You will not be able to get in the bank to take out money. Hello for bread may cost you $1000. If you can find it. If the someone who has it is willing to sell it to you. If you actually had $1000.

**Let's discuss the likelihood of the economic collapse.**

As I said before and I will say again, banks are not your friend. That will be hugely evident should an economic collapse happen and there are several things that might be the catalyst for it. Unfortunately, they will not be immediately apparent to the average taxpaying, moneysaving American.

There will be some problems globally if our money loses value.

1. Inflation starts to circle the globe.
2. Countries will fail because they do not have enough valuable metals to back their money.
3. I run on the bank for cash will cause the banks to close their doors.
4. When they close their will be no more credit.
5. The Internet will disappear causing international delays or stoppages in electronic banking.
6. Another terrorist attack, like we experienced on 9/11 in the United States, Would now disable every part of the supply chain keeping you fed in house and clothed.
7. the price of oil would skyrocket to an UN affordable amount.

8. Shipping and transportation could be delayed or even come to a grinding halt.
9. Civil unrest will lead to mass theft and uncontrollable damage and violence.
10. The government may not be able to respond to the needs of its people because they will have lost control.

**Now we will discuss the second part of this equation. How will you be protected if the economy collapses?**

When the banks closed it will come like a thief in the night and you will not get a call saying you should run down there and get your money out before it happens. This has now become a matter of survival. The best survival techniques it may seem drastic, but it is imperative that you set up and pay attention because you will not have an opportunity to do so once it starts.

I don't want this to sound like gloom and doom, but I want you to be prepared should something like this happen even on a smaller scale. We have already seen grocery store shelves empty. We have already seen gas shortages when a pipeline shuts down. We have already seen fuel prices skyrocket. But I guess you certainly didn't see anybody raising your salary to stay ahead of the raise in the cost of living.

There are a few steps you can take starting yesterday! The first thing that you should understand is you can survive it.

It will pay you to pay attention to what happens on the market and look for signs of the economy becoming unstable and the likelihood that a collapse might happen. Mark my words, it's going to happen and there's nothing you can do to stop it. But you can prepare for it.

Phase one and two of this engine that drives a collapse has already happened.

A. We are seeing record inflation causing the supply chain to falter and we are experiencing skyrocketing prices and food shortages.
B. The likelihood of a recession is right around the corner can you have heard the government and the news media talk about it. It is a direct result of inflation.

when the economy and the bank's collapse, your preparation should be in physical assets like dry goods and other things that will have low supply and high demand for. Remember when we were hoarding toilet paper. Remember when you could not find water at the grocery store. Guess what happens when the milk runs out? There have been many movies made about this exact scenario.

Movies are made based on an idea that comes from experience. We aren't going to talk about self-protection here, but it is a topic of discussion in your own circle.

- Do you have any idea where you would go?
- Should you go anywhere or stay right where you are?
- Will you have the ability to travel?
- How long would you stay if you left?
- Can you last until the crisis resolves itself?
- What if there was a medical emergency?

These are some of the questions you should ask yourself in preparation for the likelihood that a collapse will occur. The whole point of this first chapter is the demonstrate that the signs are there, and we have all seen them I choose to ignore them.

Remember when I said that my goal was to give you some education and enlightenment before it happens so that you might be prepared.

**The next chapter will highlight...**

**Who Gets A Slice of the Pie**

**What Influence and Control Mean.**

**What Mindset the Fed Likes The Best!**

**Why everyone thinks You Are The Criminal.**

# Chapter 2

## An Equal Opportunity Menace

### The Next Financial Crisis...You Ain't Seen Nothing Yet!

From first appearances everything seems OK as we've been told by the current administration and the past administration. Of course, that's what they want you to believe. The Dow Jones was up 24% last year.

The real estate index was up 7% last year. Bitcoin and other electronic money has made their debut and gathered the attention of the feds and the banks. The problem with that is that they cannot control it and they do not make any money on it. For them these are scary times.

It has taken nearly 15 years to recover from the crisis in 2007. Keep in mind that you only got about a 2% increase in pay regardless of what minimum wage was. That doesn't seem to be quite fair.

Because the unemployment rate fell to the recent low there have been fewer workers to participate in the business world for many reasons. Some of it has had to do with the coronavirus but the larger scale of it has to do with the economy stagnation.

Oh, and let's not forget student debt. My doctorate cost me $150,000. At the current rate of inflation and the looming economic collapse coupled with the current recession, it is likely that I will never be able to pay it. There is currently **more than $1.5 trillion of student loans outstanding.** Tax cuts don't translate to gross in the wages we earn. They aren't equal by any standard.

The Fed is very concerned about a meltdown caused by bigger raises in the interest rate. The Fed has assured us that employment and the economy will continue to improve if we just leave well enough alone.

**But in my opinion, it doesn't work that way.** What started in 2018 was moved to loosen the oversight of the big banks. After mortgage failures and cheap money, the bank is scared stiff to sell paper money and blow up the cash market because there's a possibility that it would cause a recession.

Well, Guess what? The Fed lowered the interest rates and debt almost doubled to about $7 trillion. Just guess who's going to pay for that?

**Who Gets A Slice of the Pie?** The Fed predicts that we are going to experience another record year of earnings. Like really?

Just because we think we were in a bubble and have a good economy, low prices, value on the dollar, and a well-run government, I beg to differ. Every bubble pops and we are in for a rude awakening. We have made concessions for US corporations to stay on the United states mainland and not move their businesses to China and Mexico and other countries. However, it came at a cost. They estimated how much they would lose in profit and the Fed I'm committed to giving him that difference to keep them here.

As things have slowed a little bit in the global economy, many U.S. companies are hanging on by their teeth. They teeter on closure and collapse. Debt is skyrocketing but being supported by the Fed. They are giving them the money that we middle class Americans have worked so hard for.

How are they able to do that? Well, they don't have to tell us how they are using our money and what concessions they have given to the central banks all around the world. You see it's not about the bank that's right around the corner. It's about banks all over the globe and in countries that are very unstable. Interestingly, thanks and their founders are unwilling to buy their own stock.

**If that doesn't scare you I don't know what does.**

Nobody in their right mind thanks that's going to end very good for anyone except those on the inside. Instead, the banks have been diverting money from their own stock portfolios to companies that have money or wage concerns. Guess who directed that.

The very people who are charged with oversight of the banks!

**What Influence and Control Mean.** As the government cracks down on people avoiding tax on their income and outright evasion of tax on their income, the penalties become higher, and the price becomes stiffer. In layman's terms that means you're going to get hit harder and they're going to take more. Many corporations haven't paid their share of taxes for many years. They've been given concessions courtesy of U.S. taxpayer.

When the government tells the banks what to do about losing money, the banks respond with changes in the interest rates paying out lower and charging more. There is no way for the average middle-class American to recover.

We can't trade enough time and labor for enough money to make up the difference.

Single handedly, without the oversight of the Fed the banks decided to lower rates to keep people from withdrawing their money. Somehow they thought that we tax Perry middle class citizens would see that as a benefit. The truth is it is simply a reduction in the value of what we already earned. This way, we are inclined to keep the money in the bank for them to use While we struggle to earn more to cover the costs of the increases in goods and services.

The banks decided to pay the Fed a visit. The topic of discussion in 2020 was how to deregulate the banking system so that they might be able to autonomously make changes without the red tape. Wow! Imagine if you could do that.

When the next financial crisis happens, it's going to be I felt more severely than even the last one. And the unapologetic banks, then become too big to fail and we end up bailing out the business where we keep our money.

**How's that for sleight of hand?** When this ride comes to a sudden stop, what we have done in the past decade is going to bring everything to light. And unfortunately, you and I are not in a position to have control over or the power to fix anything for ourselves!

**We are going to suffer the consequences.**

Please understand that I am not giving you financial advice just because this involves your money. This education is simply to bring to light what is about to happen and how you need to act and then react when it does. You will understand more when the powers that be freeze your accounts. Not because you have done anything wrong but simply because they have lost control and they want to use your money to get out of it.

## What Mindset the Banks Like The Best!

I've written several books regarding psychology and mindset because they are a huge topic of discussion especially when it is used against you. This book, cash in on the banking crisis, is the first in the crisis series of books. We will look at this topic in particular several times throughout the rest of the Crisis Series books.

In my research, I have discovered many disturbing things. One of the most disturbing things is how we are directed to do something based on what someone else thinks we should do. This is where we will talk about how your money and your finances are at huge risk to the electronic world. I wrote a book called the math of success a few years back. It is absolutely essential that you claim this book and read it thoroughly before you put another dollar in the bank.

I have several other resources that are FREE that I will rush to your doorstep in the U.S..(All I ask is to cover shipping in handling). Let's get back to the banking crisis that will happen shortly.

I am not in the habit of spreading doom and gloom, but I am in the habit of doing great research and evaluation as well as critical thinking when it comes to someone directing my actions. The banks are very good at this. It has become apparent that since we cannot save the American financial system we surely have to make efforts to save ourselves.

I am absolutely not a political person. I am however he citizen who works for the money he earns and attempts to keep every penny of it within the law.

that is why I am terrified about who the policy makers are and what influence they have over my money and your money. Although I do not have access to the policy makers had any level of the government I have however uncovered indications that I am expected to think a certain way. And I object to that.

So, let's discuss mindset and influence. I will explain the relationship between that and the complete control that the banks have. You don't want to miss this.

There is a plan in effect that will give the power behind the banks complete control of all your money. Especially during the financial crisis that's about to happen. The banks want you to think that just because you have money in their vaults, that you have some control over.

- You're not really allowed to look at it.

- There is no recourse should they make a mistake with the accounting of it.

- You can't touch it to verify that it's there.

- And ultimately, you really don't own it.

- When the collapse occurs, they will

immediately freeze every financial means you have.

- You won't be able to withdraw any money or get to your safety deposit box with your valuable documents or cash.

**The poster will read," Coming to a Neighborhood Near You".**

Although I don't know your educational status, I will give you credit for having a brain and some logical thinking. It doesn't take a genius can understand that the most prolific financial crisis ever is about to happen.

As I will detail later in this chapter, you'll discover that **the powers behind the bank will make you the criminal!**

What I experienced in 2007 was an absolute nightmare and cut me to the core. I experienced humility and embarrassment because I could not pay my bills or keep my company running. Everything I was associated with for 30 years has been in the real estate industry and it all took a nosedive in 2007. As a result, come they gladly came in took everything that I had left. Everything I had worked 30 years for. There was no mercy, no consideration, no evaluation of my ability to earn or willingness to allow me to use what resources I had left to make it better again.

**They didn't care and they let me know right up front. That was their mindset.**

That is one of the enduring moments in my life when I came to understand that I was on my own and nobody had my back. I was treated like a criminal.

As a result, I lost trust in the very banks that helped support me in my business for 30 years. In 2007 when I walked into my bank, the book was slammed shut in my face because I could no longer produce evidence of the money that I had earned!

**Go fig** I have alluded to my financial troubles in 2007 without a decent explanation of what happened. I will make it short and sweet. Well not so sweet.

I had a thriving construction business that was doing more than $2 million a year gross. I had almost $3 million in the bank save a liquid. I had two ultra-nice cars and a pickup truck. I got new ones every year thanks to my business. I was spending about $25,000 a month on material and bringing it about $50,000 a month in profit. I had planned on retirement that year, 2007. I was 50 years old.

Then, out of nowhere, the savings and loan crisis happened. It made the news at 7:00 AM in the morning. By 7:00 PM that evening I was afraid that the bank would call in the two loans I had that was supporting my purchase ability.

The banks did exactly that. It started specifically because the loans that I had were revolving and the interest rate could be changed in an hour. It also happened because they were very risky loans for the bank. Builders have a habit of going out of business overnight.

**It didn't matter that my business was 30 years old.**

To hear something that's been said before that I am sure you have heard, I was not too big to fail.

There was no one who was going to bail me out. Orders stopped coming in. There was no money to build the next house on speculation as all builders do.

About 60 days later, I was out of business. I had enough cash flow to pay my employees and to pay the last month's supply and material bills. At 120 days later, I was considering bankruptcy. Even the mention of it was enough for the bank the close the books on me. yes, you heard that right. Bad news travels fast. And in my case, it traveled even faster.

**Within six months I was homeless, foreclosed, out of business, unemployed, broke, and almost $12 million in debt.** Adding that my wife died of cancer a year and a half before that. Add widowed to the mix. I almost forgot, clinically depressed. No one to turn to, no one to talk to, no one to rely on and nothing that I had learned in 30 years could help me. By the way, all of that stuff I just told you made me the bad guy!

My banker was a very good friend who I knew for more than 30 years. When the doors closed, his statement was, “I have to do what's right for the bank”. Thank you very much...

In my case, everyone else’s actions were not quite secretive however, it was well coordinated by the bank, the lawyers, and the court. The difference between what I experienced in the crisis that we are facing is huge. Mine was on a personal level based on a national problem. In 2007 it was not only a national problem but a global problem. That's what I fear is going to occur this time had a much larger scale than last time.

So, the question I have to ask is, in fear, what will happen this time and what will the response be when this crisis becomes reality?

As you can guess, the government is not going to shell out several trillion dollars to bail out the system and the banks like they did before. They don't have the money now. But guess who does?

**You do! About 350 million of us do. Those that actually pay taxes and that they have electronic data on what money they earn, what money they save, and what money they spend.**

**Now we're back to control again.**

- It's going to come out of your 401K’s.

- It's going to come out of your savings.
- It's going to come out of your account.
- it's going to come out of your paycheck.
- Basically, it's going to come out of your Piggy Bank…no matter where you hide it. Why? Because, they have all the records. There's a huge paper trail that cannot be hidden.

It's going to be outright theft. You won't know about it because they're not going to tell you they're going to do it it's just going to happen.

**It will start with a national freeze on all bank accounts.**

The elite powers that be who oversee the banks and our financial system already have the plan in place for your money. That is why you're reading this book. To get the jump on it and prepare for yourself and your family.

I know, this sounds scary.

I know this seems alarming

I know this may frighten you.

The one thing that I absolutely know is that what I have just told you is that this is meant to protect you. What is even more scary is that Americans are completely unprepared for what's going to happen. In my book, **The Math of Success**, there are several very simple formulas to help you develop income to protect yourself in advance.

Look it up on Amazon where it is least expensive. Although, it doesn't matter what you pay for it, it is worth its weight in gold.

This is fair warning. It hurts me to think that what I know can help you and what you don't know can hurt you. I take this personally. I currently have four children. One set of twins, one son who is 13, and one daughter who is 38. I can't forget to mention my grandson who made his appearance recently.

That's why I wrote this book.

I find it very important to tell them what to expect and what will likely be the aftermath of the next crisis. I spare nothing to make light of everything that we are going to experience and many things that they will experience after the fact. I say the same things to them that I'm telling you now. They are too young to completely understand, but they are old enough to make sense of what I'm saying.

I am currently teaching them how to save their money, where to save their money, what their money can buy, what their money should buy and what their attitude should be. They are pretty bright kids and have already grasped the concept of trust and mindset. I am hoping they will not have the opportunity to be caught off guard.

**Why Everyone Thinks You Are The Criminal.**

The last concern that we need to highlight in this chapter is the bottom line. I know that my responsibility is to myself, in my family, and to my conscience.

Whether you know it or not, I hold you in high esteem as well. I believe in our Republic and keep its core values close. I understand that there are enemies within and without. Unfortunately, even the good guys sometimes consider you as the bad guys and ultimately the criminals. Simply because we want to protect what we have worked so hard to get.

If you have a single dollar to your name, I suggest that you find a way to protect it. If you don't, someone will try and take it away from you. That's just the way it is. Everyone from the Treasury Secretary of the Federal Reserve on down has a plan and the plan does not include you keeping your money

Hidden behind that seemingly genuine smile that you get, standing in front of the teller at your bank, is a subversive system that is bent on the opportunity to separate you from your money. If you don't believe me, look up the "Brisbane Rules". Very few Americans know anything about it, but every American is subject to its restrictive rules. And when the bank uses the Brisbane Rule against you, I promise it's going to hurt.

# Chapter 3
## Truth or Consequences

Here is another startling question for you to consider. **Does anyone, especially you, really know who controls your money?**

It's for certain that you don't control it is unlikely that I control it. Understanding that is a key to a great many things that I'm going to tell you next. The government does not supply you with money. They don't tell you about that in grade school or in high school or in college. The shame is that we are completely enslaved to money in order to survive.

We are afraid of not having enough of it.
We are afraid that we will not earn enough of it.
We fear that someone will take it away from us.
It consumes our lives.

**1.** When I was young, my mother's generation would always tell me to; study hard and go to college to get a degree.
**2.** Keep my "nose" clean and get a good job. (JOB...which stands for Just Over Broke),
**3.** Work hard and get your pension. (retirement).
**4.** If all goes well, you don't get hurt, you'll outlive your life insurance and eventually collect Social security.
**5.** Make sure you save enough for your

family to bury you when the time comes!

Isn't that a hoot?

It might be a "hoot", but it is within the system that they learned a long time ago. Most of which came from the GREAT DEPRESSION in the 1930s'.

Are you getting the grasp of it? They experienced a great depression. They know firsthand what happens when someone else controls you money. That's where the gangsters came from. They HATED banks. They robbed them because they hated them and the system that ran them.

**John Dillinger, Baby Face Nelson, Bonnie and Clyde, Pretty Boy Floyd, Machine Gun Kelly, and Ma Barker** all saw the result of the banks taking control and leaving you and to starve to death!...And all this for money.

In my opinion, and in my experience,

- High school was simply to learn how to go to college.
- When you went to college, it was simply to learn a trade or a skill to get the best job you could.
- Once we had the best job we could find, then we were allowed to trade time for money.

**The Big Bank Robbery!**

What is the one of the first statements made by people is, **"I didn't see that coming".**

you're going to be absolutely shocked when I make the next statement. Ultimately when the next crisis happens, you will lose 98% of your money and Everything you hold valuable!

**There has never been a truer statement made and it's based on historical evidence.** When you want your money back from the bank there is no emergency or crisis involved for them where it dictates that they have to give you your money back immediately.

Let's play, <u>what if?</u> **If you understand** that concept, you surely wouldn't be in such a hurry to give your money to the bank. In fact, if you are able to get some, if any of your money when the crisis happens, you will be counted as one of the lucky few.

**If you know that you are at the bottom** of the list to be "made whole" after your bank goes bust, it will be an act of holy miracles. Creditors come first. Trust me,

**If there is any left,** you *"might"* get what's left. Here are some questions to think about.

Do you have any idea how much money your bank has loaned out?

Do you have any idea how much money your bank has on hand at any one time? Have you ever looked at your bank's financial statements? Do you remember Wachovia bank? Do you remember Washington Mutual bank? Do you remember Landmark Bank?

> "The Financial crisis of 2007–2008 led to many bank failures in the United States. The Federal Deposit Insurance Corporation (FDIC) closed 465 failed banks from 2008 to 2012."
>
> **465 BANKS!**

**Guess who got screwed.**

**According to the treasury statistics approximately 50 banks a day fail in the United states.**

Can you handle it if your bank fails tomorrow? I consider myself pretty well prepared, however, even prepared enough to write this book but not enough to survive more than five or six months. This time the next crisis is going to be bigger and it's going to hit harder you can be left out in the cold. Not even the FDIC can cover a trillion dollars' worth of deposits. Oh yes, don't forget come the money isn't really there is it?

Also, don't forget that the FDIC only insurers about 2% have the actual money that is there.

So, when this happens come at best **you might have**

**2% of your money left because 98% of it will be gone as it is uninsured!**

Can you afford it?

When the banks and the financial system fails, as it will, you can rest assured that the bank will have your back...**NOT!** That's the reality we face. The trillions of dollars that are deposited in the bank are only insured by a very small reserve of real cash money. When this pyramid scheme crashes down on us, the banks will clear their books and start over. Just like you will have to. Just like they did in 1929.

In July of 1929 people were jumping out of buildings and committing suicide because they lost years' worth of savings. They lost everything that the industrial revolution helped them build. They lost their faith in the banking system, and they lost their trust in the government.

**How much are you willing to lose?** You don't have many options and reading this book I expect that your bank may not be one or first on the list.

If you hand me a $20 bill and trust me to hold it for you, that's exactly what I would do. With that, I am saying to you that you can trust me. It's a pretty simple concept to understand. You have no reason not to trust me, right? Even though I have control of your money there is absolutely no indication that I would do something with it or act in some nefarious way.

A big however here is, if you put your money in a bank, they control your money. They will determine if they give it back to you. They might even tell you that you can't have all of it just some of it.

The most glaring evidence to support their position is historical. Just look back 100 years. **Look at the several thousand banks that have closed since then. Look what they did with your money.** Look how the government handled the problem. Unless you're completely blind, it should be evident that the bank controls your future.

There is a whole lot more to tell you. I'll start with a common condition called, complacency. And things are going pretty well, and the job market is strong, and the pay is steady, it is easy to be lulled into a sense of comfort. This is a place you would like to stay. You think you're safe and your money is safe, and all is right with the world, **unfortunately, you could not be more wrong!** It will be an unfortunate lesson that I hope you will not have to learn.

**The word catastrophe comes to mind.**
**You must act fast, and you must act now.**
Too much money sitting in the bank it is too much money you don't own. The solution is to get control of your money and minimize your risk.

I believe that gold and silver and other precious metals might be the answer to surviving. They are not going away. Look, you, and everyone else, know something is not right with the economy right now. You may not have the time to pay much attention to it or to listen seriously about what's to happen.

Don't confuse this crisis with the government. This is strictly related to banks. Once again we have to defer to history the teach us a lesson for today.

A couple of hundred-years ago in England, the government decided that banks could be the face of the government to the people and were given the right to issue money. The problem was that there was nothing to back the money.

**Money was manufactured out of thin air.**
That's where central banking actually started. That's why we have a bank on every other corner. There were several problems that arose, and the government of the United states decided to control the money and take it away from individual banks. And from that the Federal Reserve it was developed in Georgia.
In attendance were bank presidents, government leaders and several of the richest people in the country. The meetings were held on Jekyll island on the coast of Georgia in secrecy.

They were afraid that if anyone found out about the banking bill that it would not pass the Congress and would not become law. After the bill passed, the public was told that it was in an effort to stabilize the economy. The problem with it was, it gave a small group of men the absolute power of control over money.

At the time, this was seen as a huge mistake because it would ultimately result in wealth inequality. where the central banks were the richest people gathered also. As is the cliche goes,
**"The rich get richer, and the poor get poorer."**

The bill was called "The Federal Reserve act." it was snuck into Congress attached to another bill that when passed would automatically pass the Federal Reserve act bill also. This was a classic deception. The very people who drafted the bill were also the ones that tried to fool the public stating that it would ruin the banks. Such liars and deceitful people who knew exactly what they were doing.

The bill was passed while Congress was in recess. **The Federal Reserve is now the most powerful entity in our government.** I thought you should know also that the Federal Reserve is the most powerful organization in the United States. It answers to no one.

The Federal Reserve is an independent agency standing outside the government and there is no one that has the power to even investigate or oversee anything that happens with them. The Federal Reserve is their own agency that is responsible for their oversight and investigating their issues!

**That's like the fox guarding the hen house!**

Europe has jumped on the bandwagon and now uses the same model where banking consolidation and power have become the European Central Bank. And who has the oversight and power of investigation in the European model of central banking system? Well, the European Central Bank assumes the responsibility.

Once again... **who's watching them while they are watching themselves?** What you should know is that all the currencies in the European Central Bank are backed by U.S. currency. After World War Two another system was created that gave banks even more power. It was called the **Bretton Woods System**. We'll talk about some highlights of that system but won't get deep into it because there is too much to learn and not enough room here for me to teach you. You need to look it up for yourself.

**Ain't Seen Nothing Yet.**
In 1971, then President Nixon removed the U.S. dollar from the gold standard. That means that it was not backed by an equal amount of gold. Here are some more questions for you.

1. **If the U.S. dollar is not backed** by gold as the standard what happens to its value?
2. **If the world's dollars** are backed by the U.S. dollar, what happens to their dollars because they are now backed by nothing in

return?

3. **If the trust in the U.S.** government is all that keep our dollar from loss of value, what happens when the U.S. economy tanks?

Well, here we go again. The U.S. makes more money. That means that they just print more dollar bills. If those dollars are not backed by gold it is called "Fiat" money. Fiat in Latin means "let it be so".
And then,...it is so. When the Fed says it is money then it is money. Period.

That is a problem for the other countries in the world. When our money essentially has no value because it is not backed by gold then their money becomes worth less every time we create more money.

That that translates to the entire globe using money that is backed only by faith. My friend is dangerous. **Money gets created out of thin air.** And its value is created because somebody says so.

Consider your own bank account. When you write a check to pay a bill you better darn well have money in the bank to cover that check. If you don't the check will bounce and the person you have paid will not be paid and they lose faith in you. When the Fed writes a check, there is no money in the bank. Their check is money that is just created because they say it so. Would you like to do that? Now let's imagine that you borrow money from the bank to buy your house or your car. The bank gives you a loan which is simply a paper that you sign saying that you will pay it back with interest. The bank then gives the money to the dealership or the builder for services and products rendered.

If the money doesn't actually exist, they simply create money out of nowhere. So why should you care about this or be afraid about that model? **It's because creating money out of nowhere backed by nothing and is losing its value every minute of the day, is what causes inflation.**

Then, the ball starts rolling down the hill and no one has the power to stop it. And then it becomes a crisis. Remember “truth or consequences mentioned before? Well, there are consequences, and they are and will be devastating.
And as of today,
**The US economy is now backed by debt.**

This allows banks to create a boom economy and a bust economy at will. The entire system is controlled by some very rich people at the top who controlled the banks. So now you know. There are very few people who know about this in about who controls your money. I haven't even touched the surface of this subject but know that it is absolutely crucial to your future.

For some people this is the first time learning about this. Some have known all along but choose to ignore it. Either way, make it count and use this information in good health. You don't have to believe me or let me scare you into action. Do your own research.

Here is one last bit of information that should scare you into being concerned for your future. Billionaires make money when the markets are up and when they are down. Why is that a concern? Well, **When the billionaires move their money and bet on the imminent banking crash...you need to pay attention.**

They did the same thing in 2006 right before the sub-prime crash. They made billions more on the backs of middle American taxpayers. The next one will be more than a $70 Trillion dollar collapse.

**We were forewarned.**

# Chapter 4

## The Death of Cash and Credit

The Fear of Money is Called Chrematophobia. What you may not be aware of is that you were taught to be afraid of money from the time you could understand what your name was.

From the very start, you were told to go to school, go to college, get good grades, get a good job, and honor your mother and father. And that's exactly what you have done. The problem with that scenario is, you were not taught how to live, or survive, or make it in the real world.

**From the very beginning you were taught to be a worker bee.**

There are a couple things that you were not taught in school. And I truly believe it was on purpose. From your earliest school experience, you were chastised for failure. A bad grade meant you were a failure. You were tested and failed for what you didn't know. Rarely were you ever praised for any good grades that you got. It actually seems as though the entire system teaches you how to fail and then chastises you when you do.

**What is wrong with that picture?**

Easiest explanation for that is that the powers that be actually don't want to see your success because then they lose control over your life. That, is a scary position to be in. The reason is that you can develop true wealth from your energy, experience, and education.

Your value has been exchanged for freedom, independence, and time. Control of your money is the primary focus of other people's attention. those two assets that I just mentioned, time and freedom, are the most valuable assets that you have.

**Once you learn this you'll find it easier to see that you have been fooled on a grand scale.** this is where you have the opportunity to take advantage of this crisis. This is the opportunity to transfer your wealth into the opportunity

**Getting a "money" education it is how you do that.**

The reason you're reading this book is to learn the fundamentals of how the banking system works against you. I submit that you understand the past in order to see the future. That is the entire premise of this book. Understanding what has happened before now is the crystal ball that will tell us what is going to happen. And the crystal ball is very clear. What does this have to do with the death of cash and credit? Read on and I will explain.

**You shouldn't be fooled to think that the United states currency is going to last forever.** History tells us that no country who has used Fiat currency has ever lasted very long. **You must understand the difference between money and currency** and what each one does for you and how it can be used against you. As of today, the purchasing power of money has been reduced to almost nothing. It is the 21st century "monopoly money."

a big picture explanation for the difference between money and currency starts with understanding that the things that money will buy never change. What you buy stays the same but the value of the dollar flies much less. That's how you will be controlled by the banks. As they print more and more money the value of the currency is reduced. That means simply that it buys less.

That is how the powers that be want money to work for them. The more the money supply increases the more that is sent to European countries. Eventually, all of the products and services that we import pitted against all the products and services that we export become valueless because we're also sending them the money that is used to produce them.

**The U.S. dollar needs to stay in the U.S.. According to the Fed, the more you learn about your money and the banking system the easier the harder it will be for them to keep you right where you are.**
If you think I am just fooling you, you could not be more wrong. Father in this book I will explain exactly how and what the plan looks like that has been

developed to keep you poor and poorer.

I know, you're still waiting for me to explain about cash and credit. Just hold on. I'm getting there.

You have heard a lot of people say, "there is nothing new in the world." Do yourself a favor and don't believe this. It has become very scary for the powers that be, those that run the Fed and the banks, because it has become easier to learn the things you need to know about your freedom and independence.

Not so long ago they raised the age for Social Security because people are living longer and taking more in payments then there is money going in. That is a clear example of how they changed the rules to meet the needs of money power. I like to use aviation as an example because I am very familiar with it as I spent 40 years flying airplanes and teaching other people how to fly airplanes.
If I don't know how to fly an airplane it only seems rational that it would be difficult for me to teach somebody else how to fly an airplane.

If I don't know how to manage money, it only seems rational that it would be very difficult for me to teach someone else how to manage money. These concepts are very easy to understand because they are pretty basic. So, the question is, how can anyone teaching school teach someone else about money if they themselves don't know the first thing about it?

**That's reason number one why they don't teach you about money in school. Because they have no idea how!**

Ignorance has been handed down from generation to generation have people who have no idea what they're doing trying to teach the next generation had to do something they have no idea how to do either.

Stay tuned, we're getting closer to cash and credit. The one thing that you will not know much about is that the people who have no understanding have their own finances and how it is controlled are not likely to fess up and tell you that their individual money management is a mess. That is always kept personal. Why is that always kept personal? Because everyone is humbled and embarrassed by their lack of education.

Why should we be embarrassed that we don't know where we should even start?
Did you ever wonder why a huge number of kids grow up and hate math? for the same reason that someone says I can't fly an airplane. Because they have never been taught to understand it. It certainly isn't because kids are stupid. It certainly isn't because they aren't interested. And it certainly is not because they don't have the ability to learn the basics.

It's because we don't know. I have 5-degrees including a PhD. That doesn't make me smart What made me smarter after college was spending four years learning as much as I could in my university.

**I also spent the first four years in the first-degree having time to grow up.**

I truly believe that's the only reason you go four years to college. The only reason I've learned to like math was during my first master's degree when I had to produce a financial statement for business class. It wasn't hard at all once I learned how to do it. The interesting thing was, what I really learned was, that I knew nothing about money!

I didn't know how to earn it, I didn't know how to manage it, I didn't know what to use it for that would benefit me in the best way possible and most importantly I didn't know anything about debt!.
What I came to learn the most about was the West that I knew made it easier for other people to steal my money! Please take notice that there are a lot of exclamation points after many of the sentence is in this paragraph. There is a reason for that. Because shortly now we will discuss money and credit.

I was absolutely thrilled when I got my first credit card from Exxon gas station in 1974. It was a spectacular moment when I thought that someone trusted me enough to issue me a credit card. Soon, what I would come to know was that I would pay a heavy price for that...And it didn't happen overnight. In fact, it took me about a year to increase my debt, using that card, that would stick with me for about seven years!

Before the Internet, you got your bills in the mail in envelopes every month like clockwork. What I didn't notice was the subtle opportunities I was given to use my card. **And it had nothing to do with buying gasoline.** Each bill would have a tear off sheet that was an opportunity to buy something physical. The first time I noticed it was an opportunity to buy a fully stocked, Shiny red toolbox.

That was exactly what I needed.

**More so, it was exactly what they thought I needed.** Each and every month like clockwork, I got my bill in the mail that included a different offer every month. Some of which I took advantage of because I simply had to check a box to say that I would pay for it in the future. The interesting thing was I was convinced that as a newly married guy that I needed a toolbox to take care of things in the house. It came in handy, and it was very useful, and I still have that box today that I keep just for sentimental reasons.

However, the real reason, is because that toolbox that only costs $19 in a few payments, actually ended up costing over $50 by the time I was done paying for it! **That is more-than 2 1/2 times the original cost in interest over the five years it took me to pay it off.**

**What an idiot!**

That's what the lack of education does for you. And that is exactly how the system is designed to work. That is the number one reason I learned about credit and that is how I discovered that I was absolutely scared of it. I paid for that box 2 1/2 times because I absolutely had to have it and it only took one checkbox to buy it.

We can go on and on and I can help you make sense of every purchase you have made that you should have known more about than you do. There is no more a clearer example then my first brand new car. I can say with great confidence today I will never buy a brand-new car again now that I have learned how dealerships rip you off in 20-ways more than you could have imagined.

When i told him i couldn't pay that much for a car, they worked it out. They found a way for me to pay much less every month just by extending how long I would pay for it. That's what credit does for you. That's what a good credit rating does for you. But wait!

**I didn't have any credit!** Or did I? Yes, I did remember that I had an Exxon credit card. the concept was the more I spent on the credit card and paid when it was due every month the more credit I had. Nobody taught me that and I thought that was a great concept. Until I learned that it was not the best program for me.

The few things that you are taught about money start right at the beginning. You need money to buy a roof over your head, food for your family, a car to get back and forth to work and a job you hate in the rat race trying to keep up with everybody else who's doing the very same thing because they don't know any better either.

**EDUCATION IS ONE THING BUT AWARENESS IS ANOTHER.** I promise you that money is not evil or a taboo topic. Money and credit can be very useful tools. Once you learn what not to do and once you learn what to do with it. Truth and false. Here are some truthful statements and here are some false statements. Almost all of them have been heard before. See which ones you know and have heard or believe our true.

- A penny saved is a penny earned.

- The only two things you can count on are death and taxes.

- got to spend money to make money.

- Money doesn't grow on trees.

- Nothing is free.

- If you think no one cares about you, just miss two payments that are due.

- A fool and his money are soon parted.

- If you think you need more money, you're probably right.

- Did someone say gift cards?

Here is one of the most interesting statements I have ever heard come from The Fed.

> "The largest company that buys and sells the most is the United States government. The largest company in the world that collects money in taxes and spends money earned from the people is the Central Bank."

There are more than three hidden messages in that statement.

1. The government has control of buying and selling.

2. The government collects taxes and spends money as they see fit.

3. The bank holds the money that the people earn.

4. The system that has created the above 3 manipulate buyers and sellers and earnings.

5. If the government does not have enough money, it prints more.

6. The banks control the flow of money that they hold.

7. ...and more.

Now let's talk about credit. Credit is very important to The US economy. The least understood concept of money is the formation of credit. It seems like a win-win scenario for the people. One does not necessarily have to have money to have credit.

**That in itself should scare you to death!** Remember what I said earlier about education and awareness? I am not looking to scare you I am looking to help you be more aware.

Buyers are able to buy without having money in hand I use a credit card. They pay it back with interest. There are a whole bunch of “get-chas” and “got-chas” tucked in there that we don't pay any attention to......**but are the most dangerous forms of capitalism ever invented.**

The very second that you are granted credit you are also granted debt. credit can be used in your favor and debt is used against you. Somehow that does not add up. that's one of the other reasons why people don't like math. Unless you understand it well it is absolutely frightening because you know you have no control over it.

When one person spends another person earns.

When one person earns, another person had to spend. Guess what?

We see that as a great system have money exchange and credit exchange. The problem with that is but we spend more than we earn, and we pay more than we spend. (in credit charges).

**There's a novel concept.** Spending more earned us credit. Earning more gives us the ability to pay back what we have essentially borrowed. So, what's the problem? The people that hold your money and the people that lend your money love that.

**The problem is when we aren't able to or can't earn the amount we have committed to pay.**

When you earn more and can borrow more it allows you to spend more. One more time you say, "so what's the problem"? One seems to reinforce the other. It does not seem to be a concern until something goes wrong. You lose your job or are laid off and do not have the ability to earn. Once that happens it is a death spiral that you will never escape from.

More credit debt allows ask to buy more and it takes away our ability To also buy less when we have to pay it back. So, what happens if credit did not exist?

The way the program is now if I don't earn anymore I can't spend anymore. That is a pretty simple concept, but it is also very limiting. I can't grow or improve my way of life because now I no longer have the ability to spend more than I earn.

**I love the concept of, "pay it forward."**
**I don't love the concept of why you can't earn it forward.**

The way our economy is structured now, credit has become very important to the survival of money and our way of life. It becomes a way for us to predict the future. When you use cash you understand that your debt is immediately settled. Everyone wins. When you use credit, your debt is created and is never settled until you make the next payment plus interest. That is when our concept of the differences between money and credit start.

**Money is not credit and credit is not money.** As of the minute this book was published, the United States has $29 trillion of debt. That is about $96,000 for every person in the country.

There are approximately 333 million people in the United states today. There are approximately 154 million people who worked that contribute to the federal budget. Here is the scariest number of all. **There is currently about $60 trillion that is credit extended.**

OK, so, you don't have to be a genius or have a PhD in economics to do simple math to understand that that does not add up!

Let's do some simple math.

U.S. Debt = $29-trillion dollars

U.S. Personal debt = $96,000

U.S. Workforce = 154-million people.

U.S. Credit total = $60-trillion dollars

$60-trillion divided by 154-million contributing taxpayers is...

wait for it...

wait for it...

**$389,610 dollars for every single working person in the country!**

We won't even discuss the interest, will we? The bottom line is this, there is no way on this green earth that we can survive as a country if we individually create and hold almost $400,000 in credit debt. It ain't gonna happen. There is no way that we can avoid it.

There is no likelihood that we will be able to pay it back in 1000 years if we stop making credit debt today.

Remember that I don't believe that credit is bad. I just believe that when you can't pay the interest on it back, it is bad.

When is credit good? When you buy something that helps you make more money than it cost you.

When that happens the banks increase interest rates and less people can borrow money and then they can't spend money. Has specifically for you when there isn't enough to spend you are forced to earn more. And if you can't earn more you surely can't pay on your debt in the first place. **That is how the banks control you. That is when they own you!**

Are you beginning to see how important this is to your future?

**Just wait... there is more bad news!** Guess what happens when people can't get credit? Recession is what happens. And oh yes…recession can last 8 to 10 years! What happens when we are in the belly of a recession? People are inclined to borrow more money. That is the first time you probably hear the term debt to income ratio while trying to borrow money. If you're dead is add a point greater than the ratio to what you earn, the less likely you are able to borrow money.

Remember what I said when you spend another person earns?. If you can't earn enough but continue to spend less based on credit, the entire system starts to fall apart. And when that happens...

## It becomes a crisis!

The cycle is an event that becomes vicious an unstoppable until there is nothing left.

**And that will bring us to the next chapter in this book.**

If you aren't already terrified by now, you should be.

My crystal ball says, “this is what is coming. To a neighborhood near you.”

**The Worst Economic Collapse In History Is Starting Yesterday!**

**Questions:**

- Where will the money going to come from?
- Why is most of the money in the U.S. controlled by a small number of people?
- Will the redistribution of money solve the “have and have-not” issue?
- Is this the same scenario that helped Hitler rise to power?

This is where you read on to find the answers. Don’t stop now.

## The best/worst is yet to come!

# Chapter 5

## The World Bank

### The Worst Economic Collapse In History Is Starting Yesterday!

We are now going to address some of the ifs', ands', and butts'. This chapter might be a bit controversial. It won't be heard from the media or any other source you pay attention to. And…there is a reason why.

Here are the subjects that are no big deal:

**THE GOOD.**

1. Banks are all owned by individuals, and they are in business to make money any way they can.

2. There isn't a bank that is doing poorly with your money.

3. That is about all that I could think of…and I am stretching it.

4. People will continue to work and grow and spend and earn and live and experience and enjoy life with what they have.

5. People will continue to go to movies and to

have parties and to socialize with friends and to build raise and support loved ones.

That pretty much sums it up.

**BAD.**

1. Banks are in the business to make money.
2. Banks are doing quite well with your money.
3. Banks need to keep your money in house.
4. Banks can hold your money at will!
5. The Fed raises the debt ceiling anytime
6. The Fed lends money to big business
7. The Fed makes loans to banks every day
8. Your banker doesn't want you smart.
9. Student loan debt is over $1-Trillion dollars
10. Company stock is essentially worthless
11. 1-Million companies are out of business
12. Millions are still underemployed.
13. The unemployment rate is a boldface lie.

14. Lending standards are tighter than ever.
15. Cost of living skyrockets while pay decrease. The Fed has no interest in your financial education.

Being rich has nothing to do with how much money you are in. It has everything to do with how you manage your money. We tend to believe that just a few more dollars, one more raise, a second job forfeit we just need more luck and that will be the answer to being rich.

Let's discuss all of the bad things that we numbered a page back from here and discuss why you are not rich.

- You are not rich because you have been led to believe that you are entitled to live better than you actually do.

- You are not rich because you have been led to believe that you started earning and saving money too late in your life.

- You are not rich because you have been led to believe that saving 10% of your money will give you a secure retirement.

- You are not rich because you have been told that getting a good job with benefits is the answer to a secure future.

- You are not rich because you have been led to believe that you aren't smart enough to understand the need to educate yourself about money.

- You are not rich because you have been led to believe that keeping up with your neighbors wealthy appearance is required of you.

- You are not rich because you have been led to believe that you need to buy everything that excites you except for those things that you will actually use for some benefit.

- You are not rich because you have not learned the difference between cost and value.

- You are not rich because you have been led to believe taking chances and accepting risk is bad, so you pass up opportunities.

Here are some of the

## Fundamental Consequences of the Banking Crisis Yet to Come

**Key insights:**

**When** everyone rushes to their bank to take their money out they will be caught when they learn that their money isn't there and the bank has no intention of giving them all their money

**When** the banking crisis starts in the United states it will affect every country and every bank on the globe.

**When** the banks take it upon themselves to use unethical and illegal tactics to leverage their assets, it will bolster becoming bank crisis.

**When** a banking crisis occurs as it has a river last 200 years, it spawns an even greater number of failures and reduces peoples leverage and control.

**When** the banking crisis begins, and people lose faith in the banks, investments and stock values will decrease as well. (that's what caused the crash in 1929).

**When** the Fed ignores oversight of banks, failures result in higher risks and overdependence.

**Key Insights:**

**When** banks stop lending economic growth stalls.

**When** economic growth stalls, economic liquidity falls, and unemployment goes up.

**When** banks fail in the United states, developing countries lose their role and their domestic economy.

**When** banks fail, the government increases regulation for the population.

**When** banks fail in the United states, as it did in 2008, the result was almost a complete global meltdown which destroyed several countries' economies.

I could write an entire book on simply the consequences that occur from bank failures. I won't bore you with anymore earthshattering insights. In 2006 and 2007, I actually had a part to play him is subprime mortgage failure that caused banks to fail and my own losses. I am going to bare my soul here. I am humbled by it, and I am embarrassed by it, but I do not regret it.

In 2003 when my business was doing gangbusters, I took out a loan for $1,000,000 to build my home that I would retire in. It was called a jumbo loan Anne required certain criteria that I had to meet in order to get the loan. I easily met those requirements because I was making a bunch of money and my business was doing well.

**Here is where it gets bad.** I should never have been given the loan. When running the numbers, it was obvious to me that at the current interest rate, based on what I had borrowed, added up to the fact that I could not pay back the loan. I knew it and the bank knew it; however, they chose to ignore it because it was what was called predatory lending. The mortgage companies colluded with the bank and bundled several loans from many people including me, and sold them, and made money on them without ever having to collect a dime.

There was no real regulation in the housing market, so mortgage companies chose to ignore anyone having to need 20% as a down payment and issued mortgages with zero down payment. Because of that, people who absolutely could not afford a mortgage and had no skin in the game were able to get unbelievable mortgages. And everyone was happy.

- The lending was irresponsible.
- The borrowing was irresponsible.
- The oversight was irresponsible.
- And ultimately the banks were irresponsible.

As a result, we all know what happened. Basically, there was no money to back up all of the commitments that were made. Especially the commitments that were made by the banks and the mortgage companies and the builders etc.

By the way, **there was an upside to the banking crisis and financial crisis in 2007.** Some of the greatest hustlers, thieves, embezzlers con-artists and wheeler-dealers in nefarious activity, were exposed.

And it doesn't stop there. Healthcare to a nosedive as well. There were many lost jobs. People lost their health insurance. Wages dropped significantly.

The reach of a banking crisis is unbelievable. It stretches far and wide for many years after. It is well known that taxes increase, wages decrease, wealth among the more-wealthy increases, and the decrease in people's health causes the decrease in wealth.

**Guess who suffers the most. You and me.** The impact is serious and the impact hurts. There is no end to the pain and heartache for regular people. There is no recourse for regular people.

**It all starts with greed, materialism, and selfishness.**

# Chapter 6

## The FED - Up

**Money is Good.** Anyone who does not think that money is good does not have any money hand does not have the right to comment on money.

There are many other attributes in our life for consideration however we are here to talk about money. **That is because money is the central most important aspect of all of the other of life's attributes.**

If you do not believe that that statement is true, then give up all of your savings, your income, and all the things that money has purchased for you. After that we will see exactly what your opinion of money is.

I am not here to argue whether it should be your primary focus in life or that you should worship money, however without it your life would be almost intolerable.

Many people are of the opinion that money is evil. Those that use money to help other people I would argue with you on that point. I have always said that good people will use money for good whereas bad people may use money for bad. There is some truth in the statement that money cannot buy happiness. That may be true. I think that statement requires qualification. Those people who have or has had money understand that money can solve some problems, but they also understand that money can cause problems as well. again, it depends on what you purpose money for and the decisions you make based on that.

If you are hungry or cold, money can help you control that condition. it's a very valid argument that if you had no money your life surely would not be better than it is now with money. Having money does not necessarily mean that you're required to buy gigantic homes an expensive cars and travel the world in opulence and luxury just because you have money.

Having money does, however, give you the opportunity to use it judiciously and responsibly for your wellbeing as well as all those around you.

**Thomas Jefferson, one of our founding fathers, stated that he was certain that the banks were the most dangerous institution to the liberty of the newfound country.** Money has always been a bone of contention even when the Roman Empire started losing control of the power of their money. two Roman emperors where assassinated with money being a central focus of their hatred. Although Julius Caesar gain control of the money issues, he was eventually assassinated as well because the people who wanted control of the money wanted to control him as well.

Goldsmiths worthy originators of the banking system in Rome. Paper money was invented at that time because it was easier than carrying gold and silver and jewels to use in trade for products and services.

Benjamin Franklin clearly understood that money would be the central consideration in the Revolutionary War, as it was.

In this book, I discussed with you the downside of money as it relates to banks and control. So, let's not stop there. Here are some words and concepts that you need to know of. They should strike fear in your heart if you have been paying attention at all. **I will not deny the good that money can do** but it is far overshadowed by **the bad that it has done** and will continue to do if it is not controlled.

Concepts you should know:

- BANKRUPTCY
- FORECLOSURE
- EVICTION
- UNEMPLOYMENT
- FINANCIAL RUIN

- HOMELESS
- CRASH
- TAKEOVER
- GLOBAL CRISIS
- BUSINESS CLOSED
- BANK RUN
- GOVERNMENT SEISURE
- MARTIAL LAW
- MELTDOWN
- FEAR
- PANIC

**The eventual and the coming crisis we are about to experience will make the crash of the 1930s look like a party.**

We are, or I should say the banks are, facing a crisis deeper than the world's oceans. Unfortunately, the current generation seems to have forgotten or has not lived through the prime mortgage crisis that occurred in 2007 2008. It should be evident that the future can be told just by looking at the history behind us. It seems that we will never learn and will be committed to repeat the devastating conditions of the past. Why is that?

I expect that we will never learn from the mistakes of our past because, we choose to ignore it or four get it as soon as possible because of the pain the grief and the misery that it caused. All of the conditions of the 1930s crash in the 2007 crash are excellent examples of what can happen when greed and embezzlement, and many other nefarious forms of actions that people take in their self-interest.

One of the most interesting concepts I have come to learn since acquiring a PhD is the psychology behind people thinking that they are alone in their actions.

It is as though we used complete blind this too how the actions we take affect other people around us and the entire country. It is as though people think they can do things and not be found out. It is unfortunate that people think they can do things underhanded and not get caught eventually. We are experiencing a complete erosion of professional behavior by unethical people.

This legacy that we will leave to the next generation and the following generation should be immediately studied and made aware of in order not to repeat it. However, you and I both know that is not the case and will never be. And that is sad.

## How Crisis Spreads

Certain conditions will intensify, and problems will multiply as the failure of the banking system experience is greater risk. Mortgages are going to be defaulted and people will be left homeless once again. The Fed will attempt to bail the banks out at an unbelievable cost never before seen and you and I will inherit that expense

When it gets bad enough, and that's right around the corner, you will see the rich beginning to beg for mercy. You will see the general population hands held high, begging for the minimal amount of assistance just to survive. You will find lawlessness and tragedy all around you. You will question your own confidence and your own survival. People will abandon everything they have for a slice of bread. Families will starve. The strong will still from the week. It is a condition that you do not want to experience.

Although we have not experienced much of these conditions in our lifetime there are things that have occurred in the past beyond our generation and could happen in the future after our generation.

I recall a story, about a rugby team from Uruguay, that we're traveling too chilly to participate in a game. To boil down the story, their airplane crashed on a glacier in the Andes. They spent 72 days trapped in the coldest of environments. Only 16 of them survived. The point of this story is that in the most extreme circumstances they were forced to cannibalism to survive.

This was a sensational story when I was a kid in 1972 and I remember it well. It gave me an opportunity through discussions with my parents about what cannibalism really meant. I was pretty much horrified because I could not imagine having to do that to survive.

I guess you are wondering why I would even bring that up. As I mentioned before, unless one has experienced the worst of humanity during a crisis situation, it is difficult if not nearly impossible to understand the mindset of people faced with the fear of survival and the likelihood of their death.

That story is the most gross explanation of human psychology when people panic. I have never been in that situation and hope never to be. I hope you are never in that situation. The point that I am making is, people change in a crisis situation. It is impossible to communicate or understand how someone might act. When a father is faced with the survival of his family, there may be nothing that he would not consider ensuring their survival. When a mother is faced with her children's endurance during the crisis, there is nothing that she would not consider ensuring their survival.

**The best of people will change.** Some will give up; some will try hard to endure the situation. Some will become determined, and some will stop at nothing to survive. The last of which maybe the doom and gloom during or after a crisis, but it is certainly a consideration for the rest of us who want to survive as well.

## The Prehistoric Future

Currently, anthropologists do their best to study pre-history. They study things like division of Labor, social interaction hierarchy of control and more. They split humans into two categories. One were the hunters, and the others were the gatherers. They found that CROW Magnon Man was very adept with these two groups. In the Stone Age, they used rocks and Spears to secure their food.

In the Middle Ages, somewhere between 500 and 1500 BC, people were tied to the land. There were upper class and there were serfs hello. The castle Lords would give them refuge from the elements. Sometime later, Plato, originative the concept of reality. That is when things started to go wrong.

- Ferdinand and Isabella conquered...
- Henry bourbon became king of France...
- Women in the industrial revolution...
- Mass communication was developed...
- Railroads and ask transit...

- Airplanes were invented and flew…

- Karl Marx started discussed materialism and revolution…

- Karl Marx also stated the stages of human actions beginning with slavery, feudalism, capitalism, and cannibalism…

- Lenin, Trotsky, Menshevik an others ran Russia and the communist system…

- Germany made advances on Western Europe…

- The Japanese made an appearance at Pearl Harbor…

- Ho Chi Minh forwarded the communist China way of thinking on the Asian world…

- The Gulf War send Americans into police the world's oil…

- Afghanistan becomes the center of terrorist activities…

...and here we are today. Arrived at the time now where history has been a poor teacher. There are lessons to be learned by the UN steadied actions of those before us. There is great consequence that are critical minds have failed to understand and comprehend the seriousness in the actions of previous leaders.

**There has never been a more important time in the history of The United states,** and very likely the entire planet, if we don't make ourselves aware, and educate ourselves into the failings of the people that elect to lead us.

This book, how to survive the banking crisis, **is the first in the series of 40 books that** will look carefully at the conditions that will exist if we don't learn our lessons. At the end of this book, I will give you a list of the forthcoming books that will open your eyes to what the future has to hold for you. I beg you, buy them, read them, and carry them so you will not be caught by surprise. There is not much more that I can do to impress upon you the seriousness of the subjects I have highlighted. It seems only right that I should describe to you the very thing that is presented to us today. Sometimes these things are in plain sight and sometimes they are hidden. Only individual prejudices and some collective discrimination exist among people who have the opportunity to teach us what we should know.

Unfortunately, the fact that as humans, we are subject to bias because of our education or experience. The issue becomes our concern when and individuals bias spills over into our lives. One of the primary concerns today, is that we are battling the intention to do away with cash.

In this next chapter column, I will discuss why

Why cash is in conflict.

White terrorists need cash.

Why the Fed is looking to relieve us of cash.

Why cash will disappear.

Why digital money Is dangerous.

**and many more subjects…**

# Chapter 7
## Cash Combat

There seems to be no end to it. No matter how hard I try, I can't seem to believe that people cannot see what is right in front of them. It may not be denial, but it certainly is a refusal to recognize the signs.

It seems simple to me to understand that we are moving to a cashless society and the powers that be in collusion with the banks are working very hard to make that happen. When it comes to money, the banks are the face Of the government to the public. that is just like the post office is the face of mail delivery to the government.

Once the recession is in full swing, like it is now, it's too late to try and prevent it. No one has made it official yet, but the warnings signs have been there now for several years. I said earlier that we are no longer in the industrial age, but we are now in the digital age. In the digital age there is nothing that you can hold onto. It's invisible. It is a contrived figure of your imagination. We are told what digital money is worth and there is nothing to back it up. It is worth what someone else says it's worth.

People stop buying when there is a crisis. People keep their cash in their pocket when there is a crisis. When the crisis with cash occurs, we will become a digital nation.

Why is that bad? There are no concrete boundaries with digital currency. Although digital currency is flexible it is not elastic. That means that it can change easily right before your eyes, and you have no control over it. Digital currency is easy to track. Digital currency has a very long paper trail. Digital currency can be tide to every habit that you have. Digital currency is about the flow between buyer and seller, but it has no asset of value.

**Enormous forces are at work...** To bring about the change in the banking system. It will be critical for you to know how and when this will happen in order to protect what you have. Once the change occurs, there will be no turning back. You will not have the ability to reclaim your cash. Everything you do will be subject to the rules of the bank and The Fed. This will be a gross encroachment of your rights can privilege.

**The IRS is seizing bank accounts...** unless you have been hiding under a rock, you have heard that there are proposals for the Internal Revenue Service to clamp down on deadbeat taxpayers and heavily fine anyone and everyone if they feel they have in skirting the tax laws. I promise that the good guy will get hurt too. You're either laughing all the way to the bank or you are crying all the way to the bank. Isn't that the truth?

When was the last time you went to a bank and felt comfortable? Did the tellers make you feel at ease by giving you the best service possible? Did they call you by your first name? Were they grateful for your service? The answer to those questions is a resounding yes. The reason for that is the drive to remove some of the fear that the banks represent. And you know exactly what I'm talking about.

**The cashless economy started yesterday...** Do you ever feel guilty taking your money out of the bank? Were you ever embarrassed to think that the teller is looking at your account knowing that you have no money in the bank? Do you wonder why you can never see the tellers screen? Do you ever question why, as soon as you enter the bank, they make every effort to sell you other services?

Most of the things that you don't think about when you have time think about your bank is because they do a very good job diverting your attention away from the more serious issues. Are you aware that they control every aspect of your safety deposit box? Did you know that a law has just been passed to forbid you to keep cash in your safety deposit box?

**You don't have to be a genius...** To see what is happening however you have to be awake and aware.

1. When was the last time that you saw a $2 bill?

2. When was the last time you saw a Susan B Anthony dollar?

3. Have you ever seen a $500 bill?

4. Did you know that every $20 an $100 bill has traces of cocaine on it?

5. Did you know that if you have that on your person when you are searched at the airport you can be jailed, find, and have your money confiscated?

**if you can't keep your cash safe in a bank...** If you can't keep your money in the bank, where can you keep it? Because cash is partially made out of linen, which is cloth, it does not take very long to deteriorate. What does the bank do with cash that has been used for a long time and begins to tear apart or be unreadable. The bank sends it back to the Fed to be destroyed. Why is that a problem?

Because The Fed does not replace dollar for dollar each time they destroy a bill.

**Your bank hates cash...** That sounds like a crazy statement to make but it's true. There is a great deal of work that goes into maintaining cash.

When they accept cash from you, it has checked multiple ways for it to be validated as real. Especially the $100 bill denominations. Why is that?

Money is forged all of the time quite often and very frequently. The people who forge money are getting very, very good at it. Think about it. If a man made it then certainly a man can unmake it. Or a man can remake it. It is certainly not impossible.

Do you know that if you, in the unlikely event, get a forged bill in any denomination, that when you turn it in you do not get reimbursed for it. That means if you take a $20 bill from someone and it is a forgery, you are stuck. Not only are you stuck, but the bank makes record of the fact that you turned in a $20 bill that was fake. Why would they do that?

I can tell you from personal experience, that I have accepted a forged $100 bill in a stack of $100 bills from a bank! Yes you read that correctly. The bank gave me a forged $100 bill. when I went to spend that $100 bill is when it was caught. A teller at his store marked it with a special pen to determine that it was a forgery. She confiscated the forgery and refused my purchase.

Of course, I immediately went to the bank to cry my situation and they basically ignored me saying that it was impossible. I'm here to tell you that it is not impossible. As I stated earlier, the bank would be willing to take all of the cash that you have and destroy it gladly. It would eliminate many problems for the bank.

**When you don't have cash they are in control...** And you can take that to the bank! Without using cash, then all of your transactions are digital in one form or another. The banks will have complete control all of the data and all of the information about you and your finances. If you don't think so, simply go to your local bank and ask them what information they have on you now. They would be very happy not to give you any information because they will suspect that you have come of age.

**Cash is not money..** what's the fed and the banks have declared us a cashless society, money would be completely digital every transaction would be completely traceable and would be fundamentally controlled.

Banks will have control of every single penny you have. They will be in control up every purchase you make, every transaction that you enter in, every contract that you are a party to, everything that you earn, all the taxes that you pay, and what you can buy with it.

There is an old saying, "I owe my soul to the company store." it's in a very famous song. If you've never heard of that before ask someone older than you to explain it to you. However, I will break it down in short.

When people worked for a very controlling company, the company would set up a store for their employees to purchase goods and supplies. Because workers were paid very little it was easy for the company store to inflate the cost of supplies. When workers needed supplies beyond what they earned, part of the next week's salary would already be committed to the store to pay off their debt. The problem with that is, eventually they would owe more than they make and essentially be working as slave laborers. It was a no-win situation for employees. That is the essence example of debt. Although we have not experienced that in this country in the last half century, it is something that I would surely not want to be a part of.

**Trillions of dollars in debt...** I will try and not make any political statements in this book about one party or the other or anyone like line of thinking against the other. I will simply state that there are forces in politics, they have a lot invested in building great debt in the name of progress. The point of political actions is that causes debt to have greater effect on their personal wealth then consideration for the people's wealth.

**slice of the pie...** it seems evident that powerful people get a bigger slice of the pie than anyone else That is by design. That is one of the reasons that there are no term limits in the government other than for 4-years for the president green a term limit would mean an immediate law tower and the indivisibility to build great wealth on the peoples backs.

Please don't consider this an antigovernment rant. I am simply stating the facts that you can verify easily. It is unfortunate, but these facts have a huge impact on your future. Let's get back to the banks. **We can laugh half-way to the bank.** Or we can cry all the way to the bank. If you think you are safe or insulated in some way from these nefarious actions that banks take sanctioned by the Fed, you could not be more wrong. I have a verifiable personal history that will detail otherwise. After losing everything I had worked 30 years for, **it essentially took three days to wipe out everything and put me in the street.** The system was not designed to work for me for you, but it is absolutely designed to work to their benefit. Notice I did not say against you, I said to their benefit.

Although I have no disrespect for the people that work at the bank, the tellers, and the managers, They are simply unknowing pawns ruled by the leadership who control the bank. **Influence and power…** Anytime the subject of money came up around my in-laws, my mother-in-law was famous for saying, "who do you think we are, the Rockefellers?"

That basically meant we were not rich. That basically meant we did not have any influence. That basically meant we had no power or control overall. To sum up that statement, if we had money that meant we had some power or control or influence. There are no kings, or dictators, or very wealthy individuals in my family. There are many kings and dictators and very wealthy people around the world. **Each of them has some means of power or control.** Generally, those people aren't elected but take power by force or coercion.

The next thing that you will see happening that will be very unsettling and very alarming is for the world monetary system the name itself the global central bank. When that happens, they will control the printing of money. **That's when cash will no longer be king.** That's when all the savings in the country will be a serious problem for them. That is when decisions will be made about how to deal with it. People will start hiding their cash under their mattress or burying it in the backyard. the list of alternatives to saving money that cannot be seen is very small. The powers that be understand that people will begin to do that out of fear. That's when the cashless society will be their primary focus. That is when the war on cash will begin, and it will affect the global economy.

**It will become a federally mandated Ponzi scheme.** The people with control and power will do a sleight of hand magic trick to slowly hide the cash and make you guess where it is. Ponzi schemes do not last. They are soon found out and exposed. When it comes to an end it will be dramatic. There will be panic in the streets. There may be violence and there will likely be a run on the banks. it will immediately be met with martial law to control what is about to happen.

Bankers will be hugely apologetic, but no one is going to accept it when they're hungry. But the apology will not be accepted. People will riot and attempt to retake the system create this is not a doom and gloom prediction to scare you to death, but it is easily verified throughout the last 200 years, or maybe 2000 years, as historical fact. **There will not be any more lemonade stands, garage sales, antique markets, day labor, or tips for good service paid with cash.** There will be no more under the table hidden payments because there will be no more cash. The barter system may arise to be the only form of exchange between people without the transactions being tracked. It worked for thousands of years, and it can surely work again. However, as soon as the powers to be get wind of it will be shut down and stamped out immediately.

What is going to happen to our country when this takes place? I wish I knew exactly. I am pretty sure that stocks will drop to nothing. I am pretty sure that the value of homes will drop to nothing. I am sure that it will affect the entire population of the globe. I am sure that starvation and disease home have a better hold on the health and wellbeing of the world. I am sure that the United states will not be able to lend a helping hand as they have in the past for those in need. ...And I am sure and not sure of many other things.

**The creep of control...** No, the "creep" of control is not a guy who lives around the corner. **The "creep" refers to the slow and, sometimes inadvertent, move from one place to another in slow but deliberate manner.**

That's how it happens. That's how it is sight unseen. That's when people say, "I never saw that coming". that's like it hit you like a brick between the eyes. Because it's been happening all along. It just happens so slow that you don't recognize the changes immediately. It's like your kids growing up. It seems like yesterday that they were babies and today they're grown adults. Where did the time go? How did that happen without me paying attention? Did I miss that memo? Nobody told me! Well, yes somebody did tell you. I'm telling you right now. Wake up and smell the coffee. You've taken your eye off the ball because you've been busy trying to make a living. Let's talk about sheep for a minute.

**If you had 100 sheep** in your flock and during the night a wolf snuck in and stole one, would you notice? Probably not.

**If you had 50 sheep** in your flock and during the night that wolf snuck in and stole one, would you notice? Maybe not.

**If you had 10 sheep** in your flock and during the night the wolf snuck in and stole one, you would very likely notice. In fact, you would probably have heard the wolf sneak in.

That is the closest analogy I can use to describe how the wolf is slowly but methodically stealing your sheep one by 1 without you paying any attention at all. Until it is too late, and your flock is slaughtered.

**The benefits of getting rid of cash...** There have already been laws that have been enacted to relieve you of your private property and not compensate you for it. Don't take my word for it, look it up. Look up eminent domain. Look up usury laws.

**What if I am right?** What if even some of what I say is true? Why should you rush to act?

**What we will experience shortly is more than a $100 trillion disaster.** Once this disaster escalates, there may not be any banks on every corner there were you live.

**When the dollar collapses and eventually disappears, it will be too late.** When the darkest hour that America will face is at hand where will you be? Mark my words, I am not just crying wolf. Everything I say can be verified easily. There will be no escaping what will happen, and everyone will be subject to the same rules. My message is urgent. The recession that we are experiencing now will be turned into a depression likely bigger than the last one. There will be massive deflation and unemployment. Banks will collapse like Domino's

**My biggest fear is that it's going to happen sooner rather than later.** Have you noticed that it's big becoming more difficult to find an ATM? If I am not depositing cash in the bank, the bank does not have to be open. I can use an ATM. I can even write a check and take a picture of it and send it to the bank without any need to handle cash. I have never seen a $10,000 bill and I expect that I never will.

Now that I had brought up a $10,000 bill, the government is working very hard to make much smaller transactions than $10,000 has the breaking point between whether it is reported or not. I recently heard that it was being lowered to as little as $600. Can you imagine that any purchase that you made of $600 or more would be reported to the IRS? Why would they care? **the visa cashless challenge...** Have you heard of the Visa "cashless" challenge? You haven't? I suggest you look it up. It was basically a challenge to see how long and how many times and in what form transactions can take place without using cash. That my friends, is very scary.

**The highest note dollar bill...** Why does the government continue to print more and more money when we know that is one of the reasons for a recession and has devastating effects on regular people? Because the powers that be I think that the only way to solve your money problems is with more money. **The fixed exchange rate between cash and digital money...** When we lose cash and become a digital society, who will control the exchange rate between cash and digital money? Oh, you didn't think about that did you? I promise you they did. And I guarantee you will be on the short end of that stick

**Resisting change, shaming, access, forced use, and privacy...** did you think for a minute that the powers that be, the powerful and the influential, would not stoop 2 anything to crush your movement to save your freedom? They understand that you will resist change and they will not hesitate to use shaming, access to your money, the forced use of digital currency can eliminate your privacy.

**Cash will equal crime?...** When that happens, holding cash will be a crime! Think about that one. **The smartest bankers...** The smartest bankers who control the overall system, understand where their power lies. It lies in control of your money. not controlling their own money, but in control of your access to money.

**“Give me cash or give me liberty”...**Patrick Henry of Colonial Williamsburg stated, “give me liberty or give me death”. everyone knew exactly what he meant they recognize the tyranny of the previous government. Although I am not quite ready to die for a few dollars, **the next cry might be, “give me cash or give me liberty”.** the interesting point to that statement is you may have one, but you may not have the other.

**The propaganda package...** We have changed the concept of value can it's happened right before your eyes. And it comes in the form of propaganda. In real, estate, it's all about location location, location that gives value to a property. today it's all about regulation,

regulation, regulation. The newest cashless regulation will include digital profiling. You don't think so? If all transactions are digital they will know every single thing about you. More than Google!. the form that it will take will astonish you. You, and everyone like you, carry one in your pocket or your purse. you use this tool frequently and without concern not knowing that you are giving license to every aspect of your life to nefarious people.

**Cell phones and money...** The new foggy crystal ball. cell phones don't exist as much for communication as it does for data mining. And it is big business. There are billions of dollars more in value of the data from your cell phone than there is in the cell phone itself. Even more than credit card fraud. It is the ultimate vehicle for debt slavery.

**Till debt do us part.** Death has been the greatest catalyst for ruining marriages than any other factor. Even more than infidelity. When times are good everyone is happy. When the crunch begins people start to point blame or look to shed blame. When money isn't managed well in a relationship, it soon becomes the focus of a relationship. tensions rise and distrust becomes relevant. It is the biggest unseen thief in anyone's house. **Robbers beware...** bank robber, Willie Sutton, was once asked why he continues to rob banks. He replied, "'because that's where the money is". back then you had to go where the money was stick up the bank teller with a pistol and make them feel a bag with cash. That was called a robbery. A robber did not have to have much education. Pretty much anybody could be a robber.

Today, a thief has to have some very specific technology skills in order to rob the "bank", or any other institution from the comfort of his/her couch. That theory has been tested many times so far and it seems to be working well. Now imagine that there is no cash, and all the currency is digital. The thief does not have to get his or her hands dirty. They don't have to have a getaway car. They don't have to split the money with another partner in crime. It can be done quickly and quietly and without fanfare or shooting up the ceiling of the bank. It can be completely anonymous. And it can resolve in the "take" Bing in the hundreds of thousands or millions of dollars with a keystroke.

**No more entitlement...** By any other name, entitlement may still exist but it's going to be much harder to make it happen. Take for instance, "Operation Choke Point". The federal government frequently using secret plans two either affect or control banks. Even the Fed does not like the banks. United States Department of justice has their own agenda. It was called...

> **Operation Choke Point...** "was an initiative of the United States Department of

Justice beginning in 2013 which investigated banks in the United States and the business they did with firearm dealers, payday lenders, and other companies believed to be at a high risk for fraud and money laundering".

## Selective service... No, I don't mean what happens when you turn 18 and have to register for the draft.

Even though the Department of Justice has there I on the ball looking for the various activity and illegal transactions, they are understaffed and underfunded and can't pay attention to everything. Their interest is known mostly in the continental United states. What they do does not generally include predicting terrorist attacks.

The treasury and other agencies in the government keep their eye on the economy. The intelligence community, the CIA mostly, are focused on terrorists. **So, who's keeping an eye on the dollar?**

- Who pays attention when the money supply is increased by 3.1 trillion it has been suggested?

- Who's paying attention to the trillions of debt The United states has?

- Who is paying attention to all of the American unfunded liabilities like Medicare and Social Security and student loan debt?

- Who is taking care of... Question

the things you're learning in this book is not to insight hysterical reactions, but the consequences are real. Do you trust cryptocurrencies? I am from the old school if I can't see it or touch it I don't trust it.

**Crypto currencies...trust or rust...** I firmly believe that something is valuable as money in digital form he is not valuable at all. Particularly when someone else determines what its value is without my having any input. I lost $80,000 when Enron collapsed. My loss was minimal compared to other peoples. There were people who lost multi millions of dollars in that scheme. It did not hurt any less because $80,000 to me it was as valuable as $80 million. It was to be the larger chunk of my retirement. sadly, nobody paid for it other than the people who invested in it. We paid dearly.

**Cheap labor...** I used to consider myself a valuable asset to anyone that I work for. I have made money and I have lost money. My losses have diminished the value of my labor. I am richer for the experience but poorer over the long haul for the energies that I have devoted to earning a living. **If debt were love, I'd be...**

I would be the happiest man on the planet. I might be fighting off the girls with a stick. I would be so happy money would not be a concern. I understand what debt is.

"I have used debt to make money.
I have also lost money and made debt".
**Dr. Mark Zupo**

# Chapter 8
## All the Way to The Bank

The pandemic set in motion an immediate need for access to funds. As soon as we figured out that we couldn't go out and had to be quarantined, that's when we want it out the most.

We couldn't spend money at the mall or at the restaurant, but we sure could spend money sitting in front of our computers. And because of that, online sales blasted through the atmosphere like a rocket headed to Mars. It has barely eased up. consider if you will, but the online e-learning industry will top about $328 billion before the end of 2022!

**Funny money.**

The Federal Reserve and the central bank have been analyzing technology to digitize the dollar. They want to know how it will affect the financial ecosystem and stability in the banking system. Dressed in St COVID 19 was a huge Trojan horse for the central bank to ease their way in out of necessity. The need for people to have immediate access to their funds became all too clear during the pandemic crisis. People actually increased their spending during the pandemic as opposed to reduce their spending.

Once people got there are stimulus checks directly deposited into their accounts, people who normally would not have those funds let it burn a hole in their pocket. They spent it as fast as it came in People who had plenty of funds accessible electronically use those to buy online. The stimulus Emergency relief funds came in the form of electronic cash. People did not have to work for it. And very few people will save it.

in fact, so much of it was spent that it allowed for a false boost in the economy That remained quite hollow. As soon as the money was gone, so was pulling out of the economic recession. **That set-in motion the link to digital currency and the central bank and nobody saw it coming!**

## The Grand Experiment.

What we didn't know until recently, that was the experimentation in adopting a digital dollar his much more advanced than we thought. The biggest concern among private interest is that there will not be any consumer privacy protection oversight. The Bank of Boston, Massachusetts Institute of technology, the World Bank, and other banking monsters, are testing hypothetical digital currency.

When they decide how it will be, it will be law.

So, what does that mean for you and me?

It means that owning cash can translate to being charged with a criminal offence.

**Inflation Nation** There is a term called first up forfeiture. What that means is that when all is said and done and everyone loses everything, there is a long line of people who will be paid first. Likely, that does not include you and me. A dog by any other name, is you are left out in the cold because the money will long run out before it gets to you and me.

Once under the veil of inflation, simple purchases will take on gigantic occurrences. Surveillance will increase 5-fold. You are a suspected criminal before the act of criminality just because they know enough about you to predict your future. There have been many movies made about this.

**The Big Bank Attack** Primary concern for the people is what I call the "**big bank attack.**"

The biggest lie is not telling you something that is not true, but not telling you something that is true. **Banks are really good at that.** There are passages in the constitution that protect you from the government. The federal government has only those powers specified in the Constitution and **there's no provision for a bank in there**!

Should scare you to death. Not that there is no provision for the banks there, but because the banks are free to act without constitutional oversight.

## Banks are Unconstitutional!

> Quoting Thomas Jefferson, "the constitution says, "Secretary of State Thomas Jefferson, believed the Bank was unconstitutional **because it was an unauthorized extension of federal power**. Congress, Jefferson argued, possessed only delegated powers which were specifically enumerated in the constitution. ... Hamilton conceded that the constitution was silent on banking."

The banks have become the famous,

**"Paper Trail of Tears."**

> "The **Trail of Tears** was part of a series of forced displacements of approximately 60,000 Native Americans of the Five Civilized Tribes between 1830 and 1850 by the United States government known as the Indian removal. Tribal members "**moved gradually"**, with complete migration occurring over a period of nearly a decade." Members of the Indian nations were forcibly removed from their ancestral homelands in

the Southeastern United States to areas to the west of the Mississippi River that had been designated 'Indian Territory'. The **forced** relocations were **carried out by government authorities** after the passage of the Indian Removal Act in 1830. “

**So, how safe are you feeling now?** But you wonder, how will they ever find you? For those of you that work for someone else you get a W2 showing what taxes you have paid. That is automatically reported to the government. For those of you that work for yourself or someone else as a contractor you get a form 1099 Which details what you learned in the taxes are your responsibility. An easy way to remember this is:

## Do You W2?

**1099 Isn’t Really Mine?** If you get a W2 at the end of the year, your taxes are easy to calculate as long as you do not own a business.

If you get a 1099, you get a form that describes what you learned, and the taxes are completely your responsibility. Should we transfer from cash to a digital society, there will be no need for W2s’ or 1099s’. Because you will not be able to escape your earnings any way possible. The government will know before you do.

This will help fuel the birth of the underground economy.

What other control will you learn a lot about when we transfer to a cashless economy? **The Patriot Act is the bank secrecy act…The Wikipedia definition is:**

> The Patriot Act was enacted following the September 11 attacks and the 2001 anthrax attacks with the stated goal of dramatically tightening U.S. national security, particularly as it related to foreign terrorism. In general, the act included three main provisions:
>
> - **expanded surveillance abilities** of law enforcement, including by tapping domestic and international phones.
> - **easier interagency communication** to allow federal agencies to use all available resources more effectively in counterterrorism efforts; and
> - **increased penalties for terrorism crimes** and an expanded list of activities which would qualify for terrorism charges.

If you were paying close attention when you read that, it sounds like increased safety for us. law is controversial due to its authorization of indefinite detention without trial of immigrants, and due to the permission given to law enforcement to search property and records without a warrant, consent, or knowledge.

Now as far as I am concerned, if the Patriot Act is used against potential terrorists or known terrorists in the defense of this country, I am all for it **However, we all know what happens when the power of control gets out of hand when given to anyone with equal or lesser power to police the people of this country!**

## That is unfortunate, But it is a fact of life.

> "The proverbial saying 'power corrupts; absolute power corrupts absolutely' conveys the opinion that, as a person's power increases, their moral sense diminishes."
> **1869 - John Edward Dalberg-Acton, 13th Marquess of Groppoli**

I hope that you caught the last sentence. **"Their moral sense diminishes."** This is why people fear people who have power, and influence, and money. People experience huge distress that lays hidden because of their inability to change the very thing that brings them distress.

**The 4th revolution...** We have experienced revolution before had a payday very heavy price for our involvement in it. Rarely, if ever, does anyone benefit from revolution. However, I believe that we are in the distress of the 4th revolution.

I do not believe that al Qaeda is this nation's greatest threat anymore. I do believe that the dollar will crash in a short matter of time. I write and publish this book in an effort to bring this to the attention of those that care. It seems as though, to me, that ignoring the things I have stated in this book is akin to digging the Grand Canyon deeper or longer. It seems foolish. It sounds foolish. It is foolish. It's an exercise in futility. Why would anyone print more money to get out of money problems? Why give more power to the banking system? Remember this?

**"...power corrupts; but absolute power corrupts absolutely"**

aviation, we have a saying. An accident doesn't just happen. There is a long series of events that occur long before the accident happens. And it has been proven to be exact every single time. No one gets caught in bad weather. Sources to predict the weather from point A to point B have always been there. Unfortunately, the pressure of time and money sometimes dictate foolish actions.

Airplanes don't just fall out of the sky. Mechanical failure occurs because we break the laws of the universe by producing faulty material, or faulty training, or mechanical events unseen bye scrutiny from the best mechanics. No one puts the wheels on backwards on purpose. But it happens, nonetheless.

We have not experienced the collapse yet, but there have been visible signs that the building blocks of the "money-accident" are there.

**Inclusion is delusion...** There are things that are said privately in the banking circles that are not made light of in the public circles. Bankers clearly know where we are headed and are secretly including us in the delusion.

**The marginalization award...** In this year's Darwin's awards, the biggest and shiniest award should be to the central banks. It is called the marginalization award.

**On bankers and preppers...** A prepper who is someone who believes that the world and civilization will come to a grinding halt, and they must be prepared in advance to protect themselves and their family. A prepper believes that there will be a disaster or catastrophe and they need to be prepared now. A prepper will stockpile food, water, ammunition, and other supplies. No one can agree about which disaster will happen first, but they all agree that it will happen soon

Their perception of time and the eventual result when times runs out is like the hourglass running out of sand. There is just a little bit left in the bottom. The grains of sand are moving through consistently. Our monetary system is very complex. It seemed simple to us. We go to work, and we earn money. We take that money and buy the things that help us survive. We are then depressed because there is never enough money for much else. That is a form of depression in itself

**Try on your own tyranny…** Time and money slavery…

**Again, don't misinterpret bye concept of tyranny to mean anything like an overthrow or sedition or a coup or anything like that. I am not condoning or promoting any form of or any attempt of takeover of government or bank power.**

I am however referring to the eventual collapse of our economy. All of the world's countries need energy and power. It's the supply of money is not available, in any form, then the supplies will run out. Countries with dictators will be safe and warm but their people will freeze to death or starve to death. You've seen it before, and it is likely you may see it again. it is unfortunate to start from a position far below having no debt when we are swimming in debt. There is no possible way that we can repay The United States debt. All one has to do is go to the online debt calculator to see how rapidly debt is increasing by the second. Even if we stopped the debt calculator today, **It would take six or eight generations to bring it down 50% of what it is now. Don't blame the pencil...**You can't blame the pencil for the figures. It is what it is. And unfortunately, it will never add up. This is a mathematically impossible challenge.

**Unfortunately, this makes perfect sense. (cents)**

# Chapter 9
## Common Cents

**What You Don't See.**

Karl Marx, a German philosopher, and economic critic, stated in a book that,

**"religion is the opium of the people".**

His contention was the difference between capitalism and the working people. He is recognized more for attempting to incite disagreement in the ranks of common people against religion and capitalism.

Today however there is a different drug of choice. Today we have the lottery that is visited more by the poorest people than people who have money.

The lottery, one way or another, is gambling. It is neurologically addictive.

**The lottery is also the unseen tax on the poor.** The lottery represents an opportunity to escape but provides little benefit if any to the purchasers. The people who can afford at least are the people who buy it more often. it is a hopeful attempt to escape poverty just for the possibility.

Once again it does not take a genius to understand the attractiveness of buying a lottery ticket.

People least able to dream big make every attempt but rarely makes it happen. Those that perceive themselves as the most educated with the best skills, generally, are lacking basic skills. I am not making these accusations to degrade anyone. I am stating that Those looking for clear skies end up getting their parade rained on. Respectively, the people who can't afford it least, search for it the most.

**Most people have not learned the skills that's around OPM. (other people's money).** This is one of the earliest skills I learned before making a dime. there is more power in leveraging other people's money with the same risk, or less risk then using your own money.

The problem is that we are so insecure about our own money that we ignore the opportunities using leverage of other people's money.

**We are challenged by social media watching other people flaunt what they supposedly have that we don't have.** Because of that we make foolish mistakes based on perceptions as opposed to reality. there is not much common sense and trying to keep up with anything for anybody well you don't know everything about them or their money.

- **When my grandparents were growing up**, the best they could hope for is having a business or a job.
- **When my parents were growing up**, the best you could hope for was having a television.
- **When I was growing up,** the best we could hope for was having a color television.
- **When my kids are growing up,** the best they can hope for is having a telephone.

It is virtually impossible for anyone to compete with anyone else to arrive at the same results that we think we see or have a perception of as opposed to the reality of it. The same as when I teach people my **Multiple Streams Mastery Passive Income system.**

There are **NO guarantees** of earnings anywhere remote to mine. My earnings are **NOT typical.** You are not me. **You have no idea** what I will do or not do.

**I am driven to excess** in success. **You may be excited but, not obsessive like I am.** The clearest example of that was the subprime mortgage disaster that a occurred in 2007 and 2008.

**, a clear lack of common sense driven by**

**greed.** If we somehow believe that we are poor or lesser then someone else, we do not accept it. We attempt to battle that by making decisions with our money that never work out to our advantage. Being insecure, as we humans are, we just go down the path to make more and poorer decisions again in an attempt dig us out of that negative feeling.

We will spend money to

- decrease pain,
- increase pleasure,
- save time,
- make time and
- change what is to what might be.
- RARELY, does it ever work, and it ALWAYS costs more than we expect.

We become financially desperate. People having destroyed their entire family submitting to their insecurities by taking on more debt than they could possibly payback. Student loans are a classic example of this. Brand new cars with long term payment plans or another example of this.

Payday loans are the third example of this. We can

rationalize and justify the need to do any of these things, but we just never seemed to use common sense.

Anatomical studies have shown that the size of our brain is decreasing. Although it may not be enough to see within our generation for the last two generations it is hey there are logical and biological fact. We seem to be smarter than any other creature on the planet and **yet we make the dumbest decisions to secure our future.**

The one thing we may have in our favor right now is **that the minimalist lifestyle is currently a hot topic** with the current generation. This is a valued attempt by the current generation to correct wrongs, or perceived wrongs, of the previous generation. To be exact, my generation. There are valiant efforts now to clean the ocean and restore the climate, save the whales, and reuse everything that we have. I applaud these genuine efforts.

## Right is right... or is it?

But the real question is, do we want the right thing, or the best thing, or the correct thing, or the thing that makes us happiest now? Making sure that we do not get off track, let's make sure that this applies two money and the pleasure of success.

Secondarily do we want this just for ourselves or for everyone else?

We have now come to see money equally as the most common vehicle to pleasure. Unfortunately, the value that we place on money diminishes with respect to the value we place on pleasure. Mostly, you can't have enough of either. We perceive that the greater the pleasure, the greater the satisfaction. The problem with that line of thinking is they're completely different things that have little relation to each other.

This brings us to another place. In order to derive as much pleasure as possible, you forget about the fear of risk and act in transactions that will hurt more than they will help.

You begin to ignore signs that point to danger until it is too late. If I suck just a little more than you do, I might feel good about that. If you suck just a little bit more than I do, I might feel better about that. The issue that I see with that is we are in complete denial what is really important to yourself.

"We fail to see the long-term investment in our value when we try and compare it to the short-term investment in our pleasure."

**Dr. Mark Zupo**

I have heard it said that
**"the rich are different".**
Truth is, that is correct to some degree.

Let me explain. My initial goal was to be an astronaut. Unfortunately, I discovered that I had Crohn's disease.

That was an immediate, **"sorry Pal, not going to happen". I didn't have a military background.** I was in the astronaut program for about 12 days. Basically, from the time I applied and considered as an applicant-candidate until I got the letter telling me I was not a good candidate.

Darn! My hopes were dashed. My only recourse was what I considered to be the next best thing period to become the commander of a fighter jet in the Air Force. When they found out I had been turned down by the NASA astronaut program Because I had Crohn's disease, That was an immediate, **"sorry Pal, not going to happen". I didn't have a military background.**

Darn! My hopes were dashed again. My only recourse was what I considered to be the next best thing…again. To become the commander of an airliner with a commercial airline.

When they found out I had been turned down by the Air Force program because I had Crohn's disease, That was an immediate, **“sorry Pal, not going to happen”. I didn’t have a military background.**

As I saw it, it was hopeless. However, as time went on things changed. The Vietnam era pilots were retiring several at a time. They were running out of pilots. Fortunately for me, I had already achieved a private pilot’s certificate and was heavily involved in multi engine commercial training.

(it is called a certificate and not a license) I don't know why, ask the FAA. In any case, that was entire page to make a simple point. You can't fly a jet if you don't have the proper training. It takes time. It's very involved. There is a step-by-step building block methodology.

When I teach the Multiple Streams Mastery program to my students, it follows the same rule of thumb. Building block methodology. Time and action plans. Measurement of success. It is very detailed.

The point is that, **if you become rich overnight, you will certainly lose what you have gained in no time.** And the reason is you have not been taught what to do with your recent winnings.

This has been demonstrated over and over again with people who have won the lottery who have never had a dime to their name. The average time is... **Broke in 10 years or less. Those** who are bankrupt usually are so within three to four years.

Why is that? Because it takes time and experience to learn how to manage money. As it seems to be in love come people seem to be blinded when they become rich after having never been rich or wealthy. **People become blinded to scenarios that would otherwise**

**seem crazy.** With sudden riches, people ignore the signs of being robbed blind right before their eyes. People lose the feel of common sense. What might normally be completely obvious is a fleeting thought in the background.

**People want the immediate gratification and success without learning the process to manage their gains.**

I don't want that for you. I'm willing to divulge everything I know and understand from my experience with losses and gains. It brings me great pleasure give you a moment to think about it before you act. It gives me great pleasure to keep you from making the mistakes that I did.

I want you to use common sense that will help you move from the weak person's mindset too the strong person's mindset. You have to learn to communicate to your money to do the things for you that you can't. You can't demonstrate with money that you can get the things you want until you understand about the things you need. Once you understand the value of your money beyond what pleasures you seek, then it will be worth even more.

Successful people don't become successful because they saw somebody else become successful. They become successful because they worked through and experience the process of success. Including the pain of failure during success.

You certainly appreciate the destination more if the journey was long. I know that sounds confusing but, think about it for a minute. It will make common sense.

# Chapter 10

## A Hole in My Deep Pocket

### The True Threat to Prosperity

Before we get ahead of ourselves, let's take a step back and evaluate where we have come so far.

- We recognize that something is going on and we aren't in on the secret.
- We are feeling the pain at the pump, the grocery store, shopping, and security.
- We know that our money isn't going as far.
- We see that the supplies are backed up and don't see them getting anywhere soon.
- We hear rumors of dissention and disruption and conflict.

It seems as though we Americans are worried and think that something is coming based on the political atmosphere and news casts. There is separation and division that is unsettling.

We are somewhat frightened about the economy. Systems are shutting down. Businesses are closing. People are losing their jobs. The sentiment is gray, and the mood is tense.

It is time that we focus on how to make changes that will move us forward. We need more cash. We need more freedom. We need more independence. We need it now before it is too late.

There are several economic indicators that point to a trying time ahead. There is a run-on employees leaving jobs over Covid and realizing that this is an opportunity to leave now while it is socially acceptable.

Supply chain delays and rising inflation are now the norm. The years between 2020 and 2030 may be the worst in history. The only thing that will help is a steady paycheck from an independent source that you control.

The way I see it, there is only one way to do that, and it is to build a business online ASAP while the tools are here for everyone. You have to quietly build income as a hedge against inflation, recession, and depression.

Find your best option for a business that you love. A passion that you are willing to work for.

As the mood becomes more serious, it becomes even more important to find the job you want that makes you happy and that earns you a living.

## Give Yourself Permission.

This book represents many years of hard work and mostly representations of some of my greatest failures and the success as a result. It also represents the greatest achievements of mine also. This book is more about the platform for what I believe to be huge when it comes to earning the **privilege** to be a success, whatever that may be for you too. You will find that I am a firm believer that you are in control of your destiny and only you can **give yourself permission** to be the success you want to be. Success is an option, and you don't need permission to have it. Change the victim persona to the winner persona and do it immediately. That's the first step.

I passionately believe that my success was as emotional as my losses were. Success could not have been as sweet as they are unless it cost me something along the way. That cost is the value we will talk about in more depth later. The power is yours. The power is infinite, and the power is in us all to choose the reality that we want.

**It is now time for massive, make it happen, do it now change.**
Become even more magnificent than you

are!

**Pursue your passions like there is no tomorrow.**

I want to ask the question, "Are you pursuing your dreams with all the passion you have or just along for the ride on a life you do not control?" This question begs the answer that you are not only chasing your dreams but catching them and living your life by your design! Let's examine both options and choose the one right for you. Passive income is no longer a luxury.

## Passive income is now mandatory!

I'm here to tell you that you have everything that you need to make your own reality of success a real reality. The time has never been better. The tools are easily accessible to everyone. If your passion doesn't wake you up in the middle of the night reaching for a pen or computer or notepad or recorder then you are not passionate enough! You must stretch farther than ever before; do things you have never done before and risk looking stupid to your peers before you are ready to realize that you are awesome. Accept it, wrap your arms around it and make it happen. Embrace the fear and the excitement of being awesome.

I am writing this as a citizen of the U.S.A. The greatest opportunity proving ground that has ever existed. People die trying to get here. Let me repeat that...**PEOPLE DIE TRYING TO GET HERE!** People forsake their own countries to get here. People give up everything they own, their lifestyle, their culture, their religion, their homes, their freedoms, relatives and more...**to get here.**

- The opportunities are here.
- The resources are here.
- The mentors are here.

- The technology is here.
- The financing is here.
- The support is here.
- It's all here, right now, waiting for you to get off your duff and use it.

Take advantage of it. Reach out your hand and ask for it. NOW. DO IT! And…quit finding excuses because you cannot **because you can.** And…you will.

The opportunities are revolutionary. Now is the time to start the ""YOU" revolution. (*Shameless plug…)* Here is the system I use.

## Here's Your Opportunity to Change Your Life!

**Multiple Streams Mastery™**

Click Here to Get Started

So, What the "Hello" is…

## Multiple Streams Mastery
## The Ultimate Online Passive Income System?

*Lemme 'splain it to you…*

**1. The Ultimate Online Passive Income System?**
…is the method I developed to make recurring income.

**2. What is recurring income?**
…is another way of saying residual income.

**3. What is residual income?**
…is another way of saying that the money you earn stands beside the money you work for which is, (**<u>the money you work and work and work and work for many times over for a single paycheck from a J.O.B</u>**),

Residual income comes in every month from work you produce…
**<u>just once.</u>**

There are **three main types of income** a person can earn.

A. On demand contractual.
B. On demand traditional employment.
C. Passive, recurring, residual.

**A. On demand contractual.**
A one-time job by contract is work once and get paid once. Done.

It doesn't go any further than that. If you

want more, work more.

In my book, **<u>that sucks</u>**.

**B. Active Income - On demand traditional employment.**

When you go to your work location where your job is, you are trading time and work for dollars. Traditionally, nine to five-ish. If you continue to show up every day and work for an employer, you continued to get paid once a week or every other week or so.

It is as steady as your employer says it is. Period. Most people like this because it relieves them of responsibility and usually provides insurance and some token bonuses. However, if you stop working for that employer, the paycheck stops too. If they decide that you stop working for them, the paycheck stops. So does the insurance and the bonuses if there are any. In my book,

**that sucks too**.

**C. Passive, Recurring, Residual.**
More directly named, recurring income. This is a system whereby you are continually paid even after you have stopped working! To be clear, you produce some work, (write an eBook, write a book, develop a course, develop some software, provide resources and more), ONE TIME and continually get paid repeatedly.
**This Doesn't Suck!**

The first concept goes something like this. You work, work, work, work, work, work, ***get paid once.***

**That Sucks!**

The next concept goes **exactly** like this.

**You work once,** get paid, get paid, get paid, get paid.

**continue to get paid virtually forever.**
**It is just like royalties.**

Here is something interesting to consider. Elvis, Michael Jackson, Cher, Bono, Willie Nelson, and every other superstar you can name get paid forever for one song they wrote and or sang one time…**FOREVER!**

In fact, Elvis has made more money dead than he EVER made alive!

**That is LEGACY ROYALTY!**

That is the best description of recurring income I could ever come up with.

That is also the primary opportunity for you and me to capitalize on the methods, processes, systems that can make it happen. The average Joe or Jane has the power and resources like never to make it happen.

**Welcome to the 21st Century.**

I am going to describe what working for someone else does for you.

1. “They” decide **IF** you are going to work
2. “They” decide **WHERE** you will work
3. “They” decide **WHEN** you will be paid
4. “They” decide **WHEN** you will work
5. “They” decide **HOW MUCH** to pay you
6. “They” decide **HOW HARD** you will work
7. “They” decide **HOW MANY HOURS** you will work
8. “They” decide if **YOU WILL BE REPLACED**
9. “They” decide **WHEN YOU WILL BE REPLACED**
10. “They” decide when **YOUR JOB IS ELIMINATED**
11. “They” decide **WHAT SCHOOL** your kids will go to
12. “They” decide **WHAT FOOD** you can eat
13. “They” decide **WHAT HOUSE** you will live in
14. “They” decide **WHAT CAR** you will drive

15. "They" decide **WHAT VACATION** you can take

16. **"They" decide… "They" decide… "They" decide…**

**So, what gives them all of these powers to decide for you? You gave it to them!**

I don't want to hurt your feelings but…it's true isn't it. You gave them the power when you said, "yes, I want your job." When they pay you this salary, they determine (indirectly and directly),

- **where** you can travel,
- **when** you can travel,
- **what** you can eat,
- **where** you can live,
- **what** you can drive etc.!

If you make $30,000 a year,

- **you make** about $2,500 a month.
- **You make** about $625 a week.

- **You make** about $125 a day.
- **You make** about $15.60 an hour.

Let's see, let's talk expenses.

- Car
- Childcare
- Credit Card Interest
- Doctor / Dentist
- Electric
- Emergency
- Fuel
- Gas
- Groceries
- Housing
- Insurance
- Lunches / Snacks
- Pet(s)
- Phone(s)
- Prescriptions
- Repairs
- Retirement
- Student Loan(s)

Car

a. Homeowner
b. Real Estate
c. Health
d. Life
e. Medical

...Other...

...**tell me when to stop!**

**Tell me how the "HELLO" you are going to live on that meager amount?**

Let me explain the "what do you think of it all."

**Active Income** Trading time for money. The more I want the more work it requires. Active income is where you go to work every day.

**Passive Income** A singular action for repeated results. There is no direct connection to the repeated work you must do for the results you earn.

- "What Abouts", the
- "How To's" and the
- "Why For's" of it all for you.

What if you woke up tomorrow and had money in your bank account from a small amount of **work you did once...** many months or even years ago? It is possible.

Most people get up and go to work, *but you don't have to.*

**You get PAID while you sleep**... you're different.

Instead of waking up to an alarm clock, you can do what you want, when you want and with whom you want.

That's the power of
**PASSIVE INCOME...**

**Why You Want Passive Income Streams...**

Passive income is no longer a luxury.

# Passive income is now MANDATORY!

Passive income can quickly change your life.

Most people spend most of their time working…

…And time is limited. Remember, you have 25 years OR LESS, right? Passive income provides you with the FREEDOM in your life to do the things you want to do when you want to do them.

Imagine being able to go on vacation and **getting paid**…And the best part is you're getting paid while you do the things that you want to do.

Imagine spending time with the people that you care about the most and **getting paid** while you're doing the things that want.

Building multiple streams of passive income is the key to living life on YOUR terms…The best part is...

- There are **no skills or experience required** to start
- You **don't need to spend a bunch of money**
- You can **start making money within days** of starting

- You can **scale things up to a genuinely nice six figure, passive income** within just a few short months…So, if building passive income streams is so simple, why isn't everyone doing it?

**To Successfully Build A SIX FIGURE Passive Income,**

**The Details Are VERY Important…**

**Details like...**

- Finding the right market niche to focus on.
- Choosing the passive income methods best for you.
- Getting your product / offer up and running quickly.
- Delivering value to get money flowing quickly.
- Scaling up with a **SIX FIGURE income** process.

Although the process for getting started and seeing results is straightforward…

**Most People That Try to Build Passive Income Streams Fail…**

Why is that?

It's because, there is a **PROVEN, step-by-step plan** to get results quickly. You could almost say there is a science to building passive income streams. But most people get it all wrong when it comes to getting started and seeing success building those passive income streams. It's not because it's all that hard, but because most people just try to "wing it" and just figure it all out on their own.

Plus, a lot of the information you will find out there that's freely available is just not accurate…and many people are stuck in a dead-end job with little time for anything else. That's why it seems so hard.

**When You Do Things the Right Way, You'll get Results like this…**

"Million-dollar ideas that produce million-dollar opportunities." People have "million-dollar" ideas every day but NEVER act on them because they are afraid, lack resources, lack trust, confidence, a proven system to succeed, and most of all…support!

**Do Things wrong and this is what you'll see...**

The same "crap" you have always seen no matter how hard you try. Over the years I've become an expert at building passive income streams, the right way.

That is why I want to help you. No-one helped me along the way, and it makes me mad. Not because I was jealous but just because people are afraid to share.

People fear competition. That's bull-kucky! Competition is what keeps me alert, wise, motivated, sharp, inventive, and more. I learn from competition. You should too. **NEVER fear competition.** Embrace it.

**How Can YOU Build A SIX FIGURE, Passive Income...? Read on.**

How I Built a million-dollar Online Business with Multiple Streams of Income

Dr. Mark Zupo

I always wanted to be a millionaire. When that statement was made at age 14, the second thing was that I had no idea how I was going to achieve that goal! There are misconceptions about what I believed success is for me and what you might believe that **success is for you.**

The road to "success" was fraught with potholes and barriers and took over 20 years for me to sort through like trial and error, experiences, misfortunes and delays without anyone to help or look to for guidance. Today, however, it is very different world. **Digital and online opportunity is beyond unbelievable** and provides for a multitude of mentors and coaches to look to for help and guidance. Therein the saying, "I wish...."

I first became aware of selling online in 1991. I was as green as they come back then. Although I was a bit of an entrepreneur, I had no idea how to transfer that knowledge to the Internet and sell someting online let alone make money from it. There was one thing that I did want and that was to learn as much as possible about the Internet and the digital selling process.

My first online venture was selling a $5 three-page report on…
**"How to Use Your Computer to Make Money!"** No kidding! The funny thing was...**I didn't even own a computer!**

There came a day when I realized that I needed a mentor or coach who had the experience I needed to help me become an online business owner. It was tough to find someone who would help until I met Cory Rudl in 1996. Sadly, Mr. Rudl died in a car crash in 2005. Mr. Rudl was "THE" Internet Marketing Coach of the century. He was also **my mentor** for one especially important meeting before his death that helped me to realize my potential in online business marketing. Today, **I have friends in the industry** that keep me on track, focused and provide me with the support and training to maintain my success. And trust me...I lean on them constantly!

My wife, Kathy, is the "go-to" inspiration and unbelievable support mechanism in the process of finding my success online and as a professional educator. My success is the undeniable result of her support and guidance throughout my learning and experimenting experience.

All that she does for me is reflected in my experiences, my endeavors, my products, my coaching platform and my brand...the **"SuccessMeister" of the 21st Century!'** I know it's corny but.... here's what I am going to share with you for free. Are you an entrepreneur who desperately wants to get income success? Then you need Multiple Streams Mastery...

# A

## I've Walked In Your Boots

This book is written in the first person…because I am the first person to describe my loss and success history to you. I wrote it with a degree of indignation because I am an entrepreneur and entrepreneurs find more bruises in their efforts than comfort in their creations. I know where you are and where you are coming from. My scars are a testimony to my experience and success. I wear them proudly!

# B

## Power Comes from Mentored Action

When I started as an entrepreneur in 1974, I made a statement to my friends that I would be a millionaire. Pretty bold but confident, nonetheless. I meant it with all my heart, mind, and soul. I acted after action and experienced failure after failure. Why? It was because I had no experience, no entrepreneurial education, and no model to follow. What I lacked was a mentor with experience and guidance and support that I needed to succeed.

I found him. He taught me. I made a million dollars in the second year of my newly designed business. Action is great. Informed action is greater. Mentored action is superior.

**Get a mentor.**

**Dr. Mark Zupo**
**"Mentor to Millions"**

## Introducing the Step-By-Step Guide to Passive Income Streams

**Inside, you'll discover**

- Why passive income is the best business model and how to get started RIGHT NOW...

- The simple steps to use to build passive income streams to build a consistent income and wealth

- Multiple methods for building passive streams as quickly as possible

- Which passive income stream methods you should start with if you want to get the best results as quickly as possible

- The step-by-step process to have your first passive income stream up and running THIS WEEK

- The foolproof strategy to begin growing your passive income streams on complete autopilot

- The things most people do wrong when it comes to building passive income streams and how to make sure you don't make these common mistakes yourself

- How to quickly scale up your passive income to six figures and beyond in just a few short months from RIGHT NOW

- The simple tools I personally use to automate things and make it even EASIER to setup passive income streams fast...

- **Plus, a whole lot more…**

This is the most complete, step-by-step guide to quickly building passive income streams… If you're looking to do it the right way, this is the guide for you...

**"This Sounds Great… How Much for Access?"**

Most people that try to build passive income streams find themselves wasting time and spinning their wheels...That's because they try to do it all on their own or follow bad advice that they found freely online...

This guide will prevent that from happening… When you invest in this guide today, you get…

A PROVEN plan for success that anyone can follow to start making money FAST! When you consider that you get a

TOTAL, A-Z blueprint for building a life-changing passive income...

…it would be extremely easy to put a price tag of $100, or more, on this step-by-step guide to building multiple passive income streams...

But, when you grab this today, you won't pay $100, or more.

In fact, you won't even have to invest the normal, everyday price of **just ~~$1,997.~~**

Today, you can get in at the highly discounted, one-time investment of just...
**$197 a month for the exclusive membership.**

****(P.S. We'll see who really read this book.) Hint…there's a bonus further down in the book!**

Multiple Streams Mastery™

**Whatever you do… don't wait! If you come back later, the price may be**

**higher, and I can't guarantee how long the doors to this will even be open.**

The good news is, there's no reason to wait, because I'm about to make this even better...

**When You Act Today, you'll also get These Fast Action Bonuses…**

**Fast Action Bonus #1 – Passive Income Cheat Sheet**
**(Valued at $197)**

This cheat sheet is a handy checklist that you can print out and use to easily act at every step of the process.

It breaks up the whole training into easy-to-follow steps so that you can make sure you have every single piece of advice taught in the training at your fingertips. This helps you to track your progress and will help you meet your income goals faster than you thought possible…

**Fast Action Bonus #2 – Passive**

**Income Mind Map**

(Valued at $97)

Some people learn better by looking at a mind map. This mind map gives you an overview of every step you need to apply. You can also refer to it for quick reference anytime you need it!

**Fast Action Bonus #3 – Passive Income Resource Guide**

(Valued at $997)

The Resource Guide gives you a quick point of reference to all the resources mentioned throughout the training. This makes it easy to stay on track and see results even faster!

**Fast Action Bonus #4 – Passive Income Infographic**

(Valued at $67)

If you're the type of person that likes to look at how something is done, we're including a professionally designed infographic that will show you exactly how to build your passive income empire. This makes it easy to quickly look at an illustrated guide and see what you should be doing...But please... don't wait, because I'm about to make this even easier...

**Take the Next 30 Days to Try This Out**

I don't want anything to hold you back from getting a proven roadmap to a six-figure passive income.

That's why you're going to get the opportunity to use this guide to get started and begin seeing results for the next 30 days with zero risk. After you download the guide, use what you learn inside to begin building own passive income streams that pay you while you sleep!

If for ANY reason or even NO reason at all, you're not 100% satisfied with what you learn inside, simply let me know, and I'll promptly cancel your access to the remainder of the personalized coaching.

No questions asked! I know that what you learn inside will give you everything you need to get started and start seeing results right away.

That's why I'm willing to take on 100% of the risk…

Multiple Streams Mastery™

**Get Instant Access to This Step-By-Step Guide Right Now...**

I can't wait to see you on the inside!

Dr. Mark

## Final Thoughts

What advice would I give to a beginning entrepreneur like you? The same advice I would have given me when I needed it!

**1.What I wish I knew then:**

- How to build an email list of followers loyal to you
- How to build your personal brand whatever it is
- How to focus on one thing at a time and finish it first
- How to learn as much as you can about your niche
- How to be excited always about helping other people

• How to build relationships that become friendships
• How to deliver good content that represents value
• How to be loyal to your customers because it is right
• How to be better to "mess-up than miss-out!"
• How to build trust and loyalty by respect

## 2.Drive home to your adoring public just what you stand for and how you will use it to make their lives better.

- Focus on delivering the best quality content ever
- Don't deliver anything that isn't finished
- Follow up on every complaint or concern immediately
- Treat your clients better than your friends
- Over deliver then deliver more
- Be available for questions
- It isn't all about you
- Money isn't the object

## 3.Teach what you know and become the sought-after expert.

- Focus on one area of expertise and OWN it
- Never lose track of your ability to serve others first
- Find the sweet spot and stay there
- Adjust your britches when they get too big for your butt (attitude)
- Believe in yourself unconditionally

## 4.Believe in yourself unconditionally

- If you don't believe in you then who can?
- Make your relationships your life
- Preserve your duty to deliver as expected
- Never give up on your clients or yourself

**Give yourself** permission to **succeed and fail.** Sometimes. Failure is an option and is real but then so is success, right? You will fail, and you will learn from it and move on. You can move from mediocre to magnificent at any time you choose. It is a choice that you control. The options are yours to align, adjust and mold as you see fit. You have the power to choose success and create the life of your dreams. The reality is yours. Make it happen! Be visible, be flexible and be opened to learn everything. **Do it now.**

## Multiple Streams Mastery™

Audio and video training for everyone to learn while engaged in other activities

12-Step-by-Step Dynamic Modules packed with valuable proprietary Self-Paced Multiple Streams Training

## Multiple Streams Mastery™ Membership Training Outline

# Curriculum

- **Section 1: START Here**

Lecture 1: Introduction
Lecture 2: Course Overview
Lecture 3: About Your Instructor
Lecture 4: Where to Get Support
How to Access Your Bonuses

- **Section 2: Getting Started**

Lecture 6: Basic Tools and Resources Needed
Lecture 7: Basic skills You Will Need
Lecture 8: Online Business Mindset Mastery
Lecture 9: An Overview of How Passive Income Business Works
Lecture 10: How to Ensure Your Online Business Success

- Assignment

- Resources
- Slides

➢ **Section 3: Overview of How Online Businesses Work**

Lecture 11: What is Passive Income?
Lecture 12: What is Affiliate Income?
Lecture 13: What is a Joint Venture?
Lecture 14: What is a Membership Site?
Lecture 15: How Will You Make Money in Your Online Business?

- Assignment
- Resources
- Slides

➢ **Section 4: The Basics of a Successful Legal Business**

Lecture 16: Internet Marketing Fundamentals
Lecture 17: Practical Business Information
Lecture 18: Using PayPal as a Critical Resource
Lecture 19: Setting It All Up

- Assignment
- Resources
- Slides

➢ **Section 5: Building the Platforms for Business**

Lecture 20: The Overview
Lecture 21: Your Mind map
Lecture 22: Selling Solutions to People's Problems
Lecture 23: Pricing and Payments
Lecture 24: Becoming a Membership-Messenger
Lecture 25: Access to the Bonus Training

- Assignment
- Resources
- Slides

➢ **Section 6: Understanding the Profit Engine**

Lecture 26: Building Membership Sites
Lecture 27: Understanding website development and Launch
Lecture 28: Necessary Resources for Success
Lecture 29: What People Buy, when people buy, Why they Buy
Lecture 30: Your Profit Funnel Building

- Assignment
- Resources
- Slides

➢ **Section 7: Driving Traffic**

Lecture 31: Overview
Lecture 32: Social Media Traffic Exposure
Lecture 33: Traffic Methods and Techniques

Lecture 34: Content Delivery Platforms
Lecture 35: Necessary Resources

- Assignment
- Resources
- Slides

➢ **Section 8: Critical Lead Generation to Spread Your Message**

Lecture 36: Overview
Lecture 37: Platforms
Lecture 38: Funnels
Lecture 39: Email
Lecture 40: Pre-Launch

- Assignment
- Resources
- Slides

➢ **Section 9: Scaling Your Online Business**

Lecture 41: Overview
Lecture 42: Cross-selling services
Lecture 43: Affiliates
Lecture 44: JVs' Joint Ventures
Lecture 45: High-Ticket Clients
Lecture 46: Automating Your Business

- Assignment
- Resources
- Slides

➢ **Section 10: Ready, Set Launch!**

Lecture 47: Overview
Lecture 48: Join the Team-Family
Lecture 49: Checking and Rechecking
Lecture 50: Putting It Out There
Lecture 51: Now the Real Work Starts - Delivering on Your Promises

- Assignment
- Resources
- Slides

➢ **Section 11: Critical Resources**

Lecture 52: Mind Map
Lecture 53: Slides, Transcripts, Documents, Templates
Lecture 54: Books You Need to Read ASAP
Lecture 55: Last Minute Tips and Housekeeping
Lecture 56: **Coaching - Personal and Group Opportunities

- Opportunity

➢ **Section 12: Personal Coaching with Dr. Mark Zupo**

- Who is this for?
- Why you need this now.
- What will this do for you?
- How would you use what you learn?
- What if you actually made money online?

**The opportunity to work with me to make this happen for you!** Sign Up Today At:

Multiple Streams Mastery™

# Multiple Streams

# Mastery™

Click Here to Get Started

# Conclusion

We have taken care of all you need to do with your passive income business model …. Now all you need to do is simply use these tools and tips before your competitors do that.

Don't delay…Just grab the deal!

Click on the BUY button and make money online you have never imagined.

**And there's still more to come.**

**In Addition, we are providing Bonuses!!...**
**If you buy TODAY, you get free access to 3 remarkable bonuses:**

**Bonus 1: Cheat Sheet**
**(Valued at $47)**
This cheat sheet is a practical tool that will guide you with easy-to-follow steps of

the whole training. Each and every aspect of training is broken down into easy and executable steps that will help you master the process and keep entire training at your fingertips. It makes the entire package more lucrative.

**Bonus 2: Mind Map**

(Valued at $197)

**Cover** Mind Maps will be a broad outline of the entire training program. With this handy tool, you will have a comprehensive understanding of the complete training and they will absorb the contents easily.

**Bonus 3: Top Resources Report**

(Valued at $97)

**Cover**

This is a comprehensive Research Report on Multiple Streams Mastery™ resources including: Videos, Tools, Training courses, Forums, Affiliate programs, Demographics Infographics, Facts, and

Case studies.

**So, is it worth the time and effort?** The journey to a life of freedom and flexibility starts with financial independence.

And **passive income is a HUGE part** of that. Life is infinitely sweeter on the passive online income side and this training course will equip you with the hottest passive income ideas that you can use to create reliable, long-term streams of income this year.

Just download this incredible guide to earning more money. Later in this book I will reveal all 8 income sources that I have. All 8 were re-purposed from ONE BOOK!

**You read correctly, 8 income sources from one book.**

**Our Multiple Streams Mastery™ Product comes with a special 30 Day 100% Money Back Guarantee!**
We want you to be totally psyched about our products. If at any time within 30 days of purchasing, you are not 100% satisfied, you may return it to us for a refund. No questions asked. So,
Are you ready to get started????

This really is a **Golden content!** And **deserves a HEAVY PRICE.**

**BUT** objective is to enable every entrepreneur and small business owner to **arm them with the expert knowledge** it takes to stand up to the big guys. So, we decided to offer it to you at a very

**HEAVY Discount but will be removed soon.**

**Actual Price - $4997**
**Discounted price - $1997**
**Launch Price - $1497**
**Webinar price -**

**$197 / Month!**

Here is an exclusive opportunity, limited access

**$1,497 one time**
**$799 a month 3-Pay**

---

****Exclusive Price****
**$197 a month**

Grab the opportunity with special discounts now before it is removed forever.

**Do not Wait... Get Started Today.**

## Multiple Streams Mastery™

Click Here to Get Started

**Read this carefully:**

You probably already KNOW more than enough to build a real business, the problem is, that you don't know which part of what you know is relevant to you. And until you have someone personally show you which part you need for YOU - then you will likely continue to fail to reach your goals online. The truth of the matter is this: lack of information isn't why you aren't making more money right now. You probably have hundreds of hours of training on your hard drive right now. And the truth of the matter is, when you listen to all this training, from me or anyone else, you probably think, yeah, this is great information, this could work for me.

But it doesn't.

Because you don't do it right. Or, because you don't do it at all. Because tomorrow you buy training programs to do something else. So, if information isn't the answer, what is? Why aren't most people making money online, when there is more information than ever before ready for the taking? Here's the thing, some people are. Some of my clients are. Some of my peers are. I know people who make anywhere from 10k a month to 1 million a month. What's different with these people? Why aren't most people making it, including you? One reason is that they just don't know what to do.

They know what the next step is, every single day when they wake up in the morning . . . and they do it! Let's face it, even with hundreds of hours of training on your hard-drive - you STILL don't know what you very next step is.

**(Each day you should know the EXACT next step you need to take to grow your business.)**

Confusion is what many people are teaching in the programs you buy is NOT what they themselves are doing to make a living.

*"The best way to guarantee Your success is to demand it"*
**- Dr. Mark Zupo**

# Pay Up or Pay Off?

## What would it mean for YOU?

Would it "open a gateway for you and your family to have the financial freedom to do the things you want to do"? Would your life go from "working a job to working a dream"? Would it reduce stress in your life? Would it make life easier in your family? Would it allow you to help more people? Would it "provide your family with stability, income, less worry, and options for education that would not otherwise be possible?" Would it "open up the path to a much more comfortable life and help you teach my son, his wife and my grandson the value of dedication?"

## How would YOUR life change with more income?

Here's the thing with my help you CAN get there, you can make the money you deserve. You can.

## You just should take the next step. Do it NOW!

Get started with me. Get on the phone with me for your first coaching session. You will have a breakthrough by the end of the first session. Then we will meet for 50 more hours through the course of the year. Teaching you, pushing you, directing you, molding you, giving you the exact answers, you need to build a thriving information business. By the way, it won't be easy. If you want easy, go buy another $100 training program, or another $EXPENSIVE real estate course. Easy doesn't work. It will be hard work. If you still have hair, you will pull some of it out. You will get so frustrated you won't be able to see straight. Then you will get on the phone with me, and I will tell you exactly what to do next.

**And you will do it.**

And you will have another breakthrough.

So, what is all this training worth? Let me ask you this. What SHOULD I sell it for? You see, the knowledge is in my head. But the truth of the matter is that not everyone has the success I've had. I'm what they call "not-typical" I've had results that are "not typical" See my earnings disclaimer. And the average person just doesn't get results like this. And I don't know how hard you will work, or the results you will get! But let me ask you this, would it be worth a few hundred a month to gain complete financial freedom and change your life completely? How would your life change? Would you feel like you have really accomplished something, like you have done something you could be proud of for yourself?

**Over and above all the money, would it be personally satisfying to achieve success, to be able to say…" you "did it"?**

My heart smiled when I read what a best

friend, Dave, sent me yesterday: "And some people responded that they were actually looking for what it was that I had suggested. So, it's like the pieces are already built in. It's just a matter of me putting it together in a way that gets it 'market ready'. Sometimes I have trouble staying on task. "Not having a "boss" makes it easy to get sidetracked and procrastinate. As a result, I'm not reaching my potential. I think winning the contest for the chance to work with you, under your guidance, would change all that."

**Look, this is real. You can do it. And you need my help to take you every step of the way.**

I'm going to work with you.

Get started with me today, if in 30 days, you haven't had the most amazing experience ever, and are not absolutely blown away by my training, get your money back. That's right - get started with me today - and not only will I give you your money back if you aren't blown away in the first 30 days - instead of one big upfront payment, this is easy monthly payments - so you can cancel at any time. The only thing I ask is that if you don't like the program at any point - let me know that month, I'll give your money back for the month, but if you stay in the program and take the lessons, it's not fair to everyone else to give your money back for months and months prior, is that fair?

So, there's no risk. At any point, you can cancel and get your last month's payment back. You have nothing to lose. Now, here's the way this is going to work:

It's not going to be $8,000 Or $6,000 likes similar training online Or $4,000 . . .

Instead . . . you can get started for just:

**$ 197 a month**

With no obligation . . . you can literally stop anytime you want:

## Go Here Now!

## Multiple Streams Mastery™

You will get to work with my group for one full year. You will receive one new training each week for as long as you remain enrolled (over 50 hours of group training each year, delivered weekly)

**PLUS -** you will get 10 hours of get-started-fast training immediately when you sign up. **AND -** you get to talk with me personally for up to 2 hours over the course of the next year.

The full value of all of this, if I were to sell it all separately, is **well over $100,000. AND -** it's fully guaranteed, each month is fully refundable if you do the work and at least try. You must show evidence of your work and effort. Without action there are no results.

**Now -** I must say this: if you don't do the work, you won't make the money. I am going to give you extremely specific daily instructions, exactly what to do each day to help you achieve your goals. And of course, as you are selling products and enrolling people in your own coaching program, you will be making money along the way. How would it feel to work personally with me like this?

How about you? How would it feel to work with me? Would it feel good to have someone to get on the phone with when you are stuck on something instead of trying to figure it out on your own? How would it feel to have someone look at an email, a sales page, a Tele-seminar script and say, change this, change that, so you get it right the first time, so you can make sales fast instead of having to triple split test everything? How much time would you be able to save by getting it right the first time instead of guessing and trial and error? How much faster could you achieve your goals by working with someone who's been there done that for 5 years running - and easily on track – ALREADY… (Instead of guessing??)

So, what about you?

**Are you ready?** Are you ready to change your life now - forever
(at least on this earth!!?)

Excellent - go ahead, sign up now, you will get your first training immediately when you sign up, then we will talk within the next 7 days and begin personalizing the work we do together.

## Multiple Streams Mastery™

Now here's the thing: with an offer like this, **I can't work with just anyone.** In fact, I don't want to work with everyone. So, I reserve the right to take this offer down at any time. And once I get as many clients as I can handle, I will close this offer or raise the price. If you miss out, you miss out. Frankly, **I believe this is the opportunity of a lifetime.**

**This is your year**.

This is the year to free you from the ups and downs of the financial system. This is the year to change your life and free your family. Let's get started today: Get started today for just: **$197 a month**

Multiple Streams Mastery™

It's your choice.

Perhaps you are wondering, how are we going to work together?

So, I'll share that here. But before I do, let me say this: Don't buy this because of a bunch of bullet points of all the things you are going to learn. Because I don't want you enrolling with me because you want to learn something on a list of bullet points. That's probably how you've been buying training for years now, and you keep learning bullet points, but you aren't making any more money. I don't want you buying bullet points. You are buying coaching. Working with me. Personally Frankly, exactly what I am going to teach YOU will be personalized to you only. To your personality, effort, intentions, and expectations.

## Because this is personal.

### Multiple Streams Mastery

This is going to be about getting YOU to achieve YOUR goals. And the process will vary based on what you know how to do already, how easy it is for you to do each step, and so on. So, I am going to be coaching you personally on each step of the way to help you achieve your goals. Now, how am I going to work with you?

1) We are going to meet for over 50 hours in the next year in a ridiculously small group atmosphere with about 5 other people who are also going to be building an online information business. Not only will I be working with you personally during that time, but you will also get to mastermind and network with others in the **coaching. ($50,000 value)**

2) **PLUS -** you will get 10 hours of get-started-fast training immediately when you sign up.

3) You will get to work with me personally for one full year. (Priceless)

4) You will receive one new training each week (over 50-hours of training in the first year, delivered weekly)

5) AND - you get to talk with me online for up to 5-hours over the course of the next year.

6) The full value of all of this, if I were to

sell it all separately, is **well over $50,000.**

**OR -** if you act today, you can get in for just $97 a month.

**AND -** it's fully guaranteed, fully refundable if you don't get results when you do what I teach.

HEAVY Discount **but only for the next few days.**

| | |
|---|---|
| **Actual Price -** | $2,397 |
| **Discounted price -** | $1,997 |
| **Launch Price -** | $1,497 |
| **Webinar price -** | **$197 / Month!** |

But for you an exclusive opportunity, limited access

**$1,497 one time**
**$799 a month 3-Pay**
****Exclusive Price****
**$197 a month**

## Go to This Link NOW!

www.multiplestreamsmastery.com/startnow

**Go ahead - you know this training is worth every cent,** it's 100% guaranteed . . . hundreds of past clients love my training - just do it - get signed up today, let's get you on track today!

## Get started today for just: **$197**

The ENTIRE
Multiple Streams Mastery™ System

From ~~$2,397~~

REDUCED TO one-time payment of just:

$1,497… OR **$197/Month**

**The 10-step BLUEPRINT…**
I used to build a "million-dollar" business:

**Establish a Millionaire Mindset**
This is your reality "kick in the butt"

**Specifically define your target market**
Define who you are selling to with

precision and specificity

**Become an info-product machine**
Build, build, build products, then repurpose them

**Create an irresistible and persuasive lead generating magnet**
Get their attention and deliver unbelievable value

**Create an email marketing campaign**
Capture and store permission-based opt-ins

**Convert your new leads from an opt-in squeeze page**
Publish a squeeze page that hits hard and demands action

**Drive traffic to your opt-in page with social media**
Use social media to direct attention to your site

**Monetize your list with front and back-**

**end sales.** Solve problems, create, promote, and sell what people want, offer more, offer it again. **Write and publish a best-selling book.** Build trust, establish credibility, and maintain authority and respect

The point of establishing your own list is to market to them forever.
Let's do some simple math to establish just how important everyone is to you. For every subscriber you have collected that pays you $10 dollars, it can add up to thousands very quickly.

**My job #1** is to **get you the information you need to be successful**...the secrets, which is the foundation for all you'll do as an Internet Marketer and online business owner. Most prestigious university business techniques **ruin the newest MBA graduates** from a successful entrepreneurial business life because:

- They teach people that business is tough. **Sucks!**
- They teach that you have to be special to be a businessperson. **Sucks!**
- They teach people that they can only earn small amounts for large amounts of work. **Sucks!**
- They teach people that they must work, work, work, and work to get paid once for it. **Sucks! And stupid!**

"**<u>They teach a formula for FAILURE in the true business world!</u>**"

**My job #2** is to tell you **the biggest secrets** that are worth a fortune and that you won't find in any university textbook. My job is to tell you **what topics the best sellers** are. They are the ones that will make you **a sought-after speaker and authority** to drive the kind of income you deserve.

What you have to learn are the most effective topics and procedures which can make YOU an **<u>effective, energetic, and</u>**

**high-impact product.**

## Your Call to Action

There are two important differences between motivation and inspiration. It will become important to learn what they are and many more insightful reasons that will lead you to your success. I will teach you to understand why.

- **You** are the Master of Your Success

- **You** are the Master of Your Achievements
- **You** are the Master of Wealth, Freedom and Happiness
- **You** have permission to be the success you want to be

**You** clearly have a burning desire and driving passion to learn how to be a part of this. Passion is not enough to find success, however. Many people have this passion, but few people are able to back up their passion with a quality that many people fail at – and that is **TAKING ACTION.**

Don't stop now! Most people do not even get this far!
Now it's time for you to

TAKE ACTION!

**Here is EXACTLY what to do next** Get your **STEP-BY-STEP** nuts and bolts crucial guide to actually **start making money** from your life experience, your passion, and your knowledge.

Click here to get access:
Multiple Streams Mastery™

I know this eBook has fired up the beast inside you and started you thinking. The very fact you requested this information says you have the capacity to…

Create Your Own Wealth.

So, take the plunge. Today, you will stop telling yourself you have no control over your life; and today, you will learn exactly what it means to take that control and use it to achieve success in all areas of your personal life business.

**Set a goal, plan and DO IT!**

*"The greatest manifestation of productive effort is celebrated at the Bank!"*
**Unknown**

To make it easy for you to get started, I've put together the ultimate step-by-step guide to building a life-changing passive income quickly...

Sign Up Today At:

# Multiple Streams Mastery™

# THE AUTHOR

## Dr. Mark Zupo

Dr. Mark Zupo is a self-made millionaire-entrepreneur, dynamic author of many books on leadership and online business success, inspirational speaker, and skilled businessman. Mark's programs optimize your minds, and bodies to achieve the best possible outcomes. This book will help you unlock your true potential by showing you the keys to becoming so motivated that reaching your goals will seem like the only logical result of your actions.

**Give Yourself Permission.**

This book represents many years of hard work and mostly representations of some of my greatest failures and the success as a result. It also represents the greatest achievements of mine also. This book is more about the platform for what I believe to be huge when it comes to earning the **privilege** to be a success, whatever that may be for you too. You will find that I am a firm believer that you are in control of your destiny and only you can give yourself permission to be the success you want to be. Success is an option, and you don't need permission to have it. Change the victim persona to the winner persona and do it immediately. That's the first step.

I passionately believe that my success

was as emotional as my losses were. Success could not have been as sweet as they are unless it cost me something along the way. That cost is the value we will talk about in more depth later. The power is yours. The power is infinite, and the power is in us all to choose the reality that we want.

**Mediocre to Magnificent.**

Look at a ruler and pick a number from 1 to 100. Slide your finger from 100 down to a lower number like 60. Slide the other number from 1 to somewhere around 35. Add up the distance between them and you get something like 25, right? That's about the exact number of years that we all must be at our most productive. Where are you in that process now? Year 8? Year 12? Year 20?! It is suddenly time for massive change. **It is now time for massive kick-ass, make it happen, do it now change.**
Become even more magnificent than you

are! **Pursue your passions like there is no tomorrow.**

I want to ask the question, "Are you pursuing your dreams with all the passion you have or just along for the ride on a life you do not control?" This question begs the answer that you are not only chasing your dreams but catching them and living your life by your design! Let's examine both options and choose the one right for you. Passive income is no longer a luxury.

**Life is now mandatory!**

I'm here to tell you that you have everything that you need to make your own reality of success a real reality. The time has never been better. The tools are easily accessible to everyone. If your passion doesn't wake you up in the middle of the night reaching for a pen or computer or notepad or recorder then you are not passionate enough! You must stretch farther than ever before; do things you have never done before and risk looking stupid to your peers before you are ready to realize that you are awesome. Accept it, wrap your arms around it and make it happen. Embrace the fear and the excitement of being awesome.

I am writing this as a citizen of the U.S.A. The greatest opportunity proving ground that has ever existed. People die trying to get here. Let me repeat that...

**PEOPLE DIE TRYING TO GET HERE!** People forsake their own countries to get here. People give up everything they own, their lifestyle, their culture, their religion, their homes, their freedoms, relatives and more...**to get here.**

**Here is why!**

- The opportunities are here.
- The resources are here.
- The mentors are here.
- The technology is here.
- The financing is here.
- The support is here.
- It's all here, right now, waiting for you to get off your duff and use it.

# Crisis Series Books

## From Best Selling Crisis Expert and Author

## Dr. Mark Zupo

Banking Crisis

Brain Crisis

...Coming Soon

Celebrity Crisis

...Coming Soon

Climate Crisis

...Coming Soon

Deception Crisis

...Coming Soon

Entrepreneur Crisis

...Coming Soon

Failure Crisis

...Coming Soon

Femininity Crisis

...Coming Soon

Freedom Crisis

...Coming Soon

Greed Crisis

…Coming Soon

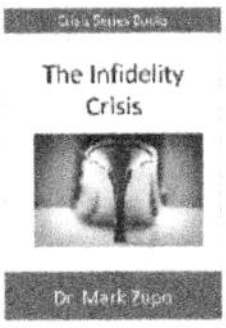


Infidelity Crisis

…Coming Soon

Killer Crisis

…Coming Soon

Lack of Logic Crisis

…Coming Soon

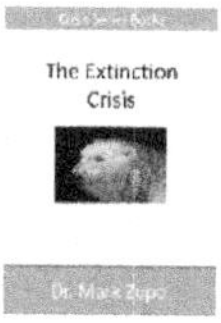


Life Extinction Crisis

...Coming Soon

Love Crisis

...Coming Soon

Masculine crisis

...Coming Soon

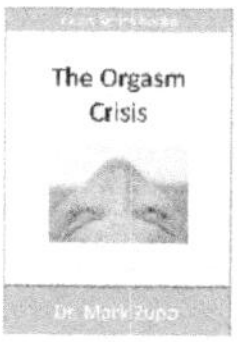


Orgasm Crisis

...Coming Soon

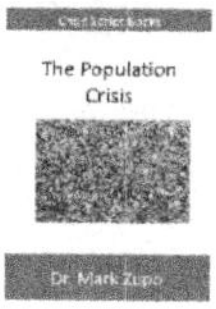


Population Crisis

...Coming Soon

Porn Crisis

...Coming Soon

Disease Crisis

...Coming Soon

Technology Crisis

...Coming Soon

Child Slavery Crisis

...Coming Soon

**<u>Remember this?</u>**

****(P.S. We'll see who really read this book.) Hint…there's a bonus further down in the book!**

**Well! Here's your reward for reading this book completely…**

**An INSTANT $50 OFF per month.**

**Instead of $197 a month**

**You pay only $147 a month!**

**…You're welcome.**

Made in the USA
Monee, IL
04 November 2026

67383942R00125